Eliza Chase Harrington

Memories of the Life of Calvin Sears Harrington

Eliza Chase Harrington

Memories of the Life of Calvin Sears Harrington

ISBN/EAN: 9783337148409

Printed in Europe, USA, Canada, Australia, Japan

Cover: Foto ©ninafisch / pixelio.de

More available books at **www.hansebooks.com**

MEMORIES OF THE LIFE

OF

CALVIN SEARS HARRINGTON, D.D.

LATE PROFESSOR OF LATIN IN WESLEYAN UNIVERSITY.

BY HIS WIFE.

MIDDLETOWN, CONN.
PUBLISHED BY THE AUTHOR.
1887

FRANKLIN PRESS:
RAND AVERY COMPANY,
BOSTON.

PREFACE.

DURING the last few months of Mr. Harrington's life, the assurance that he was rapidly hastening away gave all his words an especial value to me, and led to the habit, unnoticed by him, of committing them to bits of paper for future perusal. After he went home, I collected and copied these writings, and shared the pleasure they gave me with a few friends. Influenced by the interest they awakened, and by advice given me, I finally determined to precede them with a brief outline of my husband's history, and thus give them to the public, hoping they might assist others, fighting the same fight of faith, in winning the same final victory.

E. C. H.

MIDDLETOWN, CONN., Jan. 31, 1887.

CONTENTS.

CHAPTER I.
PARENTAGE. — CHILDHOOD. — NATURAL DISPOSITION. — EARLY HOME. — SCHOOL-LIFE. — DESIRE FOR EDUCATION . . . 9

CHAPTER II.
BEGINNING TO TEACH. — CONVERSION. — JOURNAL. — RELIGIOUS EXPERIENCE 15

CHAPTER III.
SEMINARY LIFE. — STUDENT AT WESLEYAN. — VACATIONS. — "ON THE BRIDGE." — AMBITIONS. — FEARS. — FOREBODINGS. — FAREWELLS 20

CHAPTER IV.
MARRIAGE. — TEACHING AT SANBORNTON BRIDGE. — VACATION. — NEW YEAR'S SONG. — RETURN TO SANBORNTON BRIDGE. — VARIETY OF DUTIES. — RELIGIOUS WORK. — SICKNESS 30

CHAPTER V.
RESIGNATION. — LIFE QUESTION. — GREAT FALLS. — CALL TO WESLEYAN. — COLLEGE WORK. — LATIN TRANSLATIONS. — CHURCH WORK. — "OUR COLLEGES" 36

CHAPTER VI.
PASTORAL WORK. — DIARY. — PRAYER. — EXTRACT FROM SERMON. — GENERAL CONFERENCE 47

CHAPTER VII.

EUROPEAN TOUR. — LETTERS, AND EXTRACTS FROM DIARIES, 62

CHAPTER VIII.

CALIFORNIA. — METHODIST HYMNAL. — "ADVENTUS SECUNDUS." — HYMNAL WITH TUNES. — EXTRACTS FROM SERMONS . 86

CHAPTER IX.

KARL. — BIRTHDAY POEM. — LETTERS. — DIARIES. — CLASS-MEETINGS. — SICKNESS. — VACATION. — LETTERS. — NEW-HAMPSHIRE CONFERENCE 103

CHAPTER X.

CENTENNIAL OF MIDDLETOWN. — POEM. — VACATION. — DIARY. — LETTER. — PARTIAL COLLEGE WORK. — "TO NELLIE ON HER WEDDING-DAY." — BATTLE WITH DISEASE. — WHAT IS YOUR LIFE? — OLD CHURCH. 117

CHAPTER XI.

ALUMNI MEETING AT TILTON. — EXTRACTS FROM POEM . . 127

CHAPTER XII.

EXAMINATIONS AND COMMENCEMENT. — PROFESSOR EMERITUS. — INCREASING WEAKNESS. — "THE LORD'S LEADING." — MUSIC 137

CHAPTER XIII.

FAILING PHYSICAL AND INCREASING SPIRITUAL STRENGTH. — "BORDER-LAND." — VISITS. — LETTERS. — KINDNESS OF FRIENDS. — PREACHING. — HEART-SEARCHINGS. — BISHOP FOSS. — DAY OF PRAYER. — NIGHT-EXPERIENCES . . . 145

CHAPTER XIV.

HEMORRHAGE. — PRAYER. — DAILY ROUTINE. — LETTERS. — HYMNS. — CALLS. — APPROACH OF DEATH. — DIRECTIONS. — MESSAGES. — LAST PRAYER-MEETING. — LAST SLEEP. — "INTO THOSE MANSIONS." — KINDNESS OF FRIENDS. — MEMORIAL OF FACULTY 160

MEMORIES OF THE LIFE

OF

CALVIN SEARS HARRINGTON, D.D.

CHAPTER I.

PARENTAGE.—CHILDHOOD.—NATURAL DISPOSITION.—EARLY HOME.—SCHOOL-LIFE.—DESIRE FOR EDUCATION.

IN the little village of East St. Johnsbury, Vt., close by where the noisy Moose River runs over a mill-dam, stood the brown cottage that on May 17, 1826, became the birthplace of Calvin Sears Harrington.

His mother was an invalid, of whom his only memories were of her crossing her room with feeble steps to minister to his childish wants, and sitting by her knee while she taught him with her musical voice the songs of the Church. When he was six years old, she went away to the home of the blessed.

His father was a stern, conscientious, upright man, whose love for his children was manifested in a care for their best welfare, rather than in a weak yielding to their own desires. When Calvin was four years old, his father took him to St. Johnsbury Plain, four miles from home, to a kindergarten that had been opened there. While the little fellow was busy with blocks and pictures, the parent left, and no cries availed to call him back. Calvin was boarded in a house close by, where, too small to sit with the family at table, he took his daily meals on a little tin plate at the fireside. Thus he spent his first term at boarding-school.

When a little older, his father, with great care, made him a fine cart, designed to content him in sport about home. For a while the new treasure was highly appreciated; but one day a playmate displayed the treasures of his pockets. "Boston crackers" were a greater rarity then than now, and a pocket-full of these, a nice ball of string, and some other valuable boyish traps, proved too strong a temptation; and the cart was traded off for the crackers and string. When, a few hours later, the boy offered to trade back, Calvin's father said, "*No!* Didn't you make a fair trade? Haven't you eaten up the crackers? You cannot have your cart again: it belongs to Ellery now, and I shall not make you another." The large-hearted "Ellery"—now the Hon. E. L. Hibbard of Laconia, N.H.—urged the return; but the inflexible parent would by no means allow his boy to lose this opportunity to learn that a promise once made was binding, and no reason was sufficient to induce one to break his word.

Calvin had an older brother and sister. When he was seven years of age, a new mother came to his home, bringing with her three daughters and a son. The son being about the age of the older brother, they soon began to affiliate, and the bevy of four girls found plenty in common to unite them; so the little boy of seven was left quite by himself. These circumstances developed in him a tendency to melancholy and moroseness, which so manifested itself upon his face, and perhaps in his words and acts, that a little girl, visiting in the family one day, declared innocently to the crowd, "That boy has got the *ugly*." It may well be imagined that the merriment occasioned thus at his expense did not tend to sweeten his temper. And in later years, when he was sometimes told that his disposition was naturally amiable, and he did not have to strive so hard as many others to overcome evil tempers, he would declare that naturally no one had "*the ugly*" more surely than himself, and none but himself knew how constant and severe was the battle with the Tempter, or how wonderful the grace of God that enabled him to triumph. Constitutionally he was a man of anxious care, and one must watch him through years of experience to discern that it was the indwelling Christ that kept his life calm and peaceful. He often said, "The Christian course is a warfare, and must always be, however great the grace given to aid in the fight against evil."

The same thought is frequently expressed in his diary, as: "The conflict of the world and the flesh and the Devil against God and the soul is a terrible one. If man were any thing less than he is, he would be torn piecemeal, and the object of contention would perish in the strife. But oh, how sin takes him into the ranks of evil when he consents!—and God becomes his bulwark when he flies there for refuge."

Another date has: "Battle! Battle! Christ is our Leader. Foes are within and around me. Through him I can be more than conqueror. Oh for a humble trust in my Saviour, for a meek and lowly mind, for a patient and quiet spirit! O Lord, sanctify thy servant. Give me a holy heart.

"Fight, fight, fight! I am tired of it. It is of no use to quarrel with the decrees of law, wherever they originate. Submit is the word. Man is a living interrogation-point, and very crooked he is."

Father Harrington's cottage-home stood at the base of one of the greenest of Vermont hills; and his farm stretching back behind it showed on the lowlands well-cultivated gardens and fields, where digging and sowing and raking and hoeing furnished plenty of opportunity to teach a boy that labor was both necessary and honorable. Wide pastures farther up the ascent gave room for berry-picking and cattle-driving, and the heavy woodland at the top furnished chopping and sledding for winter's occupation. The beautiful grove of maples, called "First Woods," half-way up the hill, was attractive for its ice-cold spring, that furnished the house below with water, and was the rallying-place for the whole herd of cattle as they came each night in procession down the well-beaten path. In the season for farm-work this Vermont boy was never unoccupied, except when on some rare occasion, having persuaded his father to give him a "stint," he had with youthful zeal accomplished two hours work in one, and so saved the afternoon for fishing, gaming, or other of the myriad boy-sports from which labor had by no means taken his relish.

But there would sometimes come an end to the rush of farm-work. Father Harrington had provided for all such emergencies. Beside the stream in front of the house stood a tannery and a small shoe-manufactory; and over the dashing current an old bark-mill hung, where hours otherwise unoccupied were spent in grinding bark. This was a work Calvin especially hated, as the dust filled his nose and throat, while the din of the machinery, as the old mill creaked and groaned at its labor, was any thing but pleasing. Still hour after hour, keeping the hopper filled to its utmost, he contented himself by leaning from the window over the falling water, and raising his voice to its highest pitch, vying with the sounds about him, as he sang all the songs of his boy-programme, including many of the hymns of the hymn-book.

The evenings were mainly spent in reading, the facilities for which he used every means to gain. The old family library was culled over and over, and all the variety from Arabian tales, and Robinson Crusoe, to Rollin's Ancient History, and John Bunyan's dream, were eagerly devoured. By some boy-trade he became possessed of his first appreciable sum of money. Richer than Rothschild in feeling, he walked the next leisure afternoon four miles to the nearest book-store, and invested this fortune in three volumes of the British poets, — Pollok's "Course of Time," Milton's "Paradise Lost," and Young's "Night Thoughts," which furnished the following winter evenings' delightful occupation, and, carefully treasured, became the nucleus of his future library.

A few weeks of district school each summer, and a long term in winter, he enjoyed with ever-increasing zest. At the age of thirteen, he spent his first term at old Newbury Seminary. Two of the girls of his home "boarded themselves" there, and a boy was a convenient member of such a family. Frequently in autumn he attended a term of select school in his native village. So, little by little, he was laying a foundation for an education that from his early childhood he had earnestly coveted. But he began to grow impatient at the long delay, as the years of farming and tanning went on, and he became aware that he was reaching up to manhood, and his progress toward the goal of his ambition was scarcely perceptible.

In the winter of 1844 and 1845 he taught his first school in Bath, N.H., and the following spring spent his well-earned money in a term of study in St. Johnsbury Academy, then in charge of Professor Colby.

The following summer, coming in one day from farm-work, discouraged with the kind of life he was leading, and quite out of sorts with the world in general, he called out to his father, who sat quietly reading, "Father, I wish you would buy me a watch." — "Well, I shall not," replied the wise parent. "Then I wish you would send me to school," Calvin continued. After a few minutes of silence, his father answered, "If you will work well this summer, you may go to school this fall; then, if you can teach in the winter, you may go to school as long as you can pay your own way." This was the "proclamation of emancipation" to the petitioner. He mowed and raked, and tumbled and pitched off, during the remaining haying and harvest season, with a courage and will he had never shown before.

CHAPTER II.

BEGINNING TO TEACH. — CONVERSION. — JOURNAL. — RELIGIOUS EXPERIENCE.

AFTER enjoying the fall term at the academy at St. Johnsbury Plain, he engaged a school for the winter in "Ross District," Lower Waterford, Vt., and then really began the work of teaching that only ended with his life. During this winter, boarding at some distance from his work, he spent the hour of intermission in his schoolroom. Soon after the term commenced, he began to look around for something to occupy this comparatively quiet and leisure hour. Finding at hand only the Bible, aside from ordinary text-books, he bethought him that though he had always read and heard the Bible read daily, had studied it also from his childhood in Sunday school, still he had never given it a really thoughtful perusal. After turning over the leaves a little, he decided that he would spend this leisure midday hour in reading carefully and thoughtfully the Psalms of David. Putting this resolution in practice, he found his attention absorbed and his interest fastened more and more on those wonderful truths and poetical utterances. The words of inspiration did not fail to reveal their power, and to stamp their impress on the young inquirer's heart.

One evening, after his duties for the day were ended, as he sat alone in the little chamber at his boarding-place, he thought of his Christian home, of the house of God where he had year after year sung songs of worship, of the sabbath school and its instructions, of the many lives that he knew as having a Christian faith and experience that he had not; and he asked himself, "Why am not I a Christian?" He could give no answer. His conscience told him that it was not only the most reasonable thing to serve God, but that the Author of his being and the Source of all his blessings had a rightful claim upon his service, that heretofore he had utterly disregarded. He saw the unjust position he had been holding, and deliberately decided he would no longer be inconsistent with himself. Since he believed he owed his life to his Maker, he would henceforth pay his honest dues to Him who held this infinite claim. Having deliberately made up his mind thus, he kneeled, and formally gave himself to God; then retired to rest with a heart calm, unmoved, but satisfied in having done the present duty.

The week ended, and he went home, as usual, to spend the sabbath. He found the little village of East St. Johnsbury all awake to the interests of the Christian religion. Daily meetings were being held, and on Saturday evening he made his way to the chapel where the villagers were assembled. The earnest prayers and songs of praise to the great Father, and the simple testimonies to a faith in Christ Jesus that brought peace to troubled hearts, all had their convincing effect on one already decided to do the bidding of the Divine Master; so that, when an opportunity was given, he scarcely needed the earnest glance of a dear brother to induce him to bow at the altar where public consecration was made to God. After the prayers, his voice calmly told the purpose of his life henceforth. And on Monday morning he went back to his school, full of a new zeal and readiness to be all for Christ; saying to his brother, on the way, "I don't know but I shall some time find it is my duty to become a preacher of the gospel."

Six months later, June 28, 1846, this entry was made in his journal: —

"For the first time in my life, I have to-day partaken of the holy sacrament. I can scarcely describe my feelings when kneeling at the table of my Lord. They were of a mingled character. I felt that I was unworthy to take even the crumbs that fall from his table. I felt humble and solemn and penitent. At the altar my prayer was for pardon through Jesus' death and sufferings, and a perfect cleansing from all sin through the efficacy of his blood. Upon my seat afterward, my inward prayer was, 'Hereafter, O Lord, enable me to do all thy righteous will.' I do desire to be more holy. I am far from being satisfied with my present situation. I am not filled with all the fulness of Christ, not devoted enough to his cause, not trusting enough in his merits, not enough dead unto sin and alive unto God. Oh that from this time no power of temptation may cause me to fall, no artifice of the Devil may lead me astray from the path of duty and the way of peace!"

There was so little emotion, so little of the frequently attendant joy, at the time of his conversion, that sometimes, in the few years following, he wondered if he could be professing a faith which had no experimental reality. This fear at times was painful to him, when he compared his own experience with the more emotional one of some of his associates. In the fall of 1847 he attended a camp-meeting at which the power of the Holy Spirit was especially manifest. There he sought a satisfactory evidence that the real work of God was wrought in his own heart. One evening, as he was praying for this in the midst of a little circle in one of the tents, his prayer was suddenly changed to praise. The quiet tones that so uniformly told his desires to God were replaced by hallelujahs and shouts of "Glory!" For some minutes the place was indeed "shaken where we were assembled," as in the olden time, while the presence and power of the Holy Ghost was manifest to all.

In describing afterward his feelings at that time, Calvin said, "I cannot tell how it came : I only know that while I prayed it seemed to fall on me as a shower, and to cover me from head to foot." That experience he always loved to recall as a time when God gave him an especial token and proof of his sonship in revealing to him a little of the power and glory of his grace. It was the only time in all his experience when the manifestation of his emotion could have been called *noisy*. Though often in later years he was filled with the conscious presence of Christ, he expressed it quietly, — sometimes in tears of joy, sometimes in glad songs of praise.

The following New Year's Day, Jan. 1, 1848, his diary has this entry : —

"Believing, as I do, that 'to fear God and keep his commandments is the whole duty of man,' I have thought it best to form some rules for my own government, and to prescribe for myself some duties which it shall be my endeavor to perform.

"1. I will endeavor to *be* a *Christian*,— to love God

supremely, to perform every Christian duty made known to me, and to '*grow* in *grace* from *day* to *day*.'

" 2. I will for this end set apart at least two seasons every day for secret prayer, self-examination, and reading the Scriptures.

" 3. I will never parley with the *adversary*, but endeavor to *shun the very appearance of evil.*"

This short but comprehensive code of rules, so conscientiously adopted, was never afterward renounced.

CHAPTER III.

SEMINARY LIFE. — STUDENT AT WESLEYAN. — VACATIONS. —
"ON THE BRIDGE." — AMBITIONS. — FEARS. — FOREBODINGS.
— FAREWELLS.

IN the spring of 1846, Calvin entered the college preparatory course in old Newbury Seminary. Here he worked with most indefatigable zeal in his studies; keeping his health good meanwhile by vigorous engagement in baseball, football, snowball, climbing "old Pulaski," and taking long and rapid walks through all that mountain region.

From the time of his conversion, though he prized as highly as one could all intellectual opportunities, and set himself conscientiously to improve all that came within his reach, yet above these he set the culture of his spiritual life. The weekly prayer and class meetings he never neglected. The plea of "no time" was never thought of; because, from the outset, he planned time for them, just as he planned time for his daily meals and recitations. This rule of life, that never allowed religious duties to yield place to any thing else, early well established, in later years made duty a delight.

He always found time also to seek out and try to help those who were forgetting these higher interests, and in those years his success in this work was marked. Here, as everywhere, his love for music was rendered useful. Often an otherwise weary hour of summer midday was made cheery in that old boarding-house, as, surrounded by a crowd of fellow-students, he led their voices in chorus, or sang song after song, accompanied by the little old-fashioned melodeon which he held upon his knees.

In August, 1848, having completed his course of preparation for college, he started in the old-time stage-coach on his journey to Middletown, Conn.

Arriving a stranger in the city late in the afternoon, he was set down, by the hackman, at the fence-gate on High Street, opposite the two old stone piles that then constituted the nucleus of the present elegant line of university buildings. He went cautiously up the long walk, and reverentially looking in at the open door beheld the janitor, acting president for the vacation not yet ended. He called for a room, and was shown one in which the pile of furniture of all sorts, set as if ready for the auctioneer's block, reached the ceiling. But in the midst of it was one bed dressed for use. He was allowed to occupy that for the night. It is doubtful whether his waking or sleeping dreams were most tantalizing. The ideas he had cherished of Wesleyan University, as the centre of all that was attractive and elevating, seemed to be some nightmare of the past; and the memory of home, with its cosy chambers, well-furnished tables, and loving hearts, was very bright beside this damp-walled, unlighted room.

But "tired nature must have her dues:" so, despite the racings of rats and mice and some lesser animals, he spent a few hours in sleep, rising early to make preparation for the opening term. Dr. Olin, as president of the university, answered all his previous ideas of a college president. Other members of the faculty he soon came to regard with the highest deference. And though the general surroundings, and the intellectual character of many of the students, greatly disappointed him, yet he prosecuted the four-years' course with constantly increasing appreciation not only of the opportunity afforded him to gain the book-knowledge he had so long coveted, but to gain also many other things from the privileges of college life. Thenceforth his alma mater was cherished by him with all the enthusiasm of a child who knows the value of real parental care. His eye would kindle with excitement, and his voice grow eloquent, whenever, in after-years, he used his influence to send pupils to old Wesleyan. The beauty of the city, the charming walks and delightful views of the surrounding country, the culture of the social world there, and the delights of college companionship, all were added to the strong testimonials of merit he gave to the faculty of the university, and the various advantages and privileges connected with the institution. He was an ardent lover of his college society. He often said, "To no one thing in all my course do I owe more than to the help I received from the Psi Upsilon Fraternity." He loved it as long as he lived; and one of the last messages from his lips was sent to "our boys," — as he loved to call them, — urging them to a constant course of right-doing and patient working.

As everywhere and always, he made college a workshop. "College life has more truth than poetry in it," he used to say. "It is drill, drill, from Monday morning till Saturday night; and then it is, with me, sing, sing, on the sabbath; so I am about as tired on Monday morning as on Saturday night." In those days, chapel devotions occurred at six, and recitations commenced at a quarter past six. This steady plodding from day to day he relieved, as often as vacation came round, by visits to his childhood home, where he was always gladly welcomed. Arriving unexpectedly at one time, after the family had retired for the night, he climbed to his own chamber-window, and entering enjoyed a fine sleep. When the large family circle, to which two younger sisters and a brother had been added some years before, were all seated at breakfast, he walked quietly into the dining-room, and claimed his place among them. The joyful breakfast over, word went to the eldest brother, — who had married, and lived next door, — that his help was wanted to get a strange animal out of the woodshed. Arming himself with a long pole, he at once obeyed the summons, and, putting his eye to a crack in the out-house door, beheld the young collegian demurely seated on the wood-pile. The racings and wrestlings, the laughter and chatter that followed, went far towards conquering all dyspeptic tendency, and preparing for another year of vigorous study.

Calvin found here also various means of combining good-doing with health-gettting. In the summer of 1849, a new church was being built in the little village; and, adapting himself to the occasion, he became first carpenter by trade, and worked with hammer, square, and plane; then painter, and put on the two coats of white that finished and beautified the new house of worship.

Standing one day on the bridge that spanned the noisy stream just below the old bark-mill, calling back the days of yore, he composed one of his earliest poems, which he entitled, —

ON THE BRIDGE.

Through a village in the mountains
   Where my boyhood days were passed,
Rushing down from far-off fountains
   Runs a river clear and fast.
O'er a chasm deep and narrow,
   Just below the whitened fall,
Where the torrent like an arrow
   Shoots along the spray-wet wall,
There a rustic bridge is hanging
   With its airy swaying floor,
High above the waters, spanning
   All the gulf from shore to shore.

Bending there low o'er the railing,
   In my boyhood days of dream,
I have spent the hours in sailing,
   Sailing *up* the hurrying stream;
For to wayward fancy's seeming,
   Gazing on the flood below,
Through the air I flew in dreaming,
   While the waters ceased to flow;
Yet forever when I landed
   From my voyage up the flood,
There my phantom ship lay stranded
   Where the bridge had always stood.

Such is life: across time's river
   Thus for each a bridge is thrown;
Bending o'er the railing ever,
   Each, enraptured, gazes down,
And with 'wildered sense believing
   That we fly past vale and hill,
In our dreams ourselves deceiving;
   In our places stand we still.
Thus "the thing that hath been shall be;"
   Only man grows old and gray,
And when death shall close our dreaming,
   Only *he* shall pass away.

The four years in college were in many respects years of enjoyment and satisfaction, and yet of much anxious care. Several things conspired during the time to foster Calvin's natural tendency to melancholy. Exceedingly sensitive, his dread of censure was a continual torment. He longed for the approval of his friends, and, indeed, of all. To feel that any human being had any other than kindly feeling toward him, made him wretched. During his first year he wrote: "It is natural for me to look upon the dark page of life's book. What troubles me would not trouble another. Molehills to some are mountains to me. 'Trifles light as air' are often magnified to things of great importance. It was always so. A word, a look, a little act, an imagined neglect, or a seeming attention, will cause a world of joy or grief, as the case may be."

His ambition amounted almost to a passion, and was a demon he fought through all his life; and college rivalries did not tend to lessen its strength. To stand second in a class of twenty-four, was a fear that often tormented him, and a fact, at last, that seemed to him an almost unendurable disgrace. The drama "Cromwell," for the junior exhibition, he prepared with encouraged ambition; but of the Latin salutatory for graduation he wrote: "I have written my Latin jargon short and sweet. I hate it. Well, never mind; it may be all for the best, I presume it is. Oh, I have been, and am, I fear, very proud and ambitious. When I look at my own heart, I see a thousand manifestations of vanity and ambitious desire that I fear are wrong. How much *may* I be ambitious? I want to do just right."

His naturally doubting mind received little help from

the influences about him. Another letter says, "Help me by your prayers. You know I am of a doubting nature. Strong faith I am almost an entire stranger to. I sometimes think it is harder for me to be a Christian than for any other human being." Again he says, "I was sad last evening from a hundred rushing thoughts, and yet scarcely one was distinct and definite. I had just returned from class-meeting, and I always feel sad after communing with my own heart an hour. Oh, how much wickedness is there! how much coldness, and ingratitude, and pride, and passion! I felt sad that I was not rid of the doubt and darkness of scepticism, which so greatly hinders me from that religious enjoyment I so much long for, — that I was so weak and useless a professor of religion. How overwhelming is the sense of my utter nothingness, and destitution of mental or spiritual endowments and acquisitions, especially spiritual, as it sometimes comes upon me!"

The great question of his life-work was continually recurring to him; and a fear that he should be unable in any position to meet life's stern demands and God's righteous dues, made him often despondent.

Once he wrote: "You cannot tell how I shrink, at times, from the future, — how I fear to enter upon its trials and responsibilities. I always did dread the post of responsibility. I fear I may not meet the expectations of those who are gazing upon me and criticising. I shrink greatly from the voice of censure, and the frowns of a cold, heartless multitude." Again, "Oh, the future! It is well, no doubt, I cannot fathom it. No doubt it is wise that the Infinite has thrown around it the curtain of thick darkness. Yet who does not often long to read the doom of destiny? . . . Well, let us console our hearts with the recollection that 'He doeth all things well.' If we cannot live by sight, let us live by faith. I am thankful, that, although the destiny of this life is shrouded in impenetrable gloom, yet far behind the dark cloud-banks we can catch glimpses of the streaming light of the future life. Oh for strength to weather every storm on life's ocean, that we may at last emerge into the sunlight of God's everlasting presence!"

His financial condition troubled him. At the end of the first year he found his small resources exhausted. He found also that it was impracticable to spend, as he had planned, each winter term out of college. He tried to utilize vacations in various ways. Once he attempted to canvass for periodicals, but those who knew him would be likely to smile at the thought. Unwilling, as he always was, to ask a favor, he felt, in this position, like a street beggar; and, never voluble with his tongue, the flippancy of a successful canvasser was an acquirement he could not gain.

He taught singing-schools with success during the winter vacations, and once made an arrangement to give a course of concerts with a friend. After the first evening's experiment, which proved quite satisfactory, the man, for some reason, was unable to meet further engagements; therefore the vacation tour was an embarrassment instead of a help. This led him to abandon all further efforts to pay by the way; but, obtaining a life-insurance policy for the safety of his creditors, he thereafter borrowed money, and gave his whole care to study.

About the beginning of the last term he wrote: "I have just been making a rough calculation as to the amount of cash I must have to meet the term's expenses. I presume I can borrow it, as I have heretofore. It will leave me, when I graduate, six hundred dollars in debt; but I am determined not to be blue about it. I have many things to encourage me. My friends will sympathize with me, if they cannot help me. I shall be through college with health, and hands, and a disposition to work. My Father's eye is upon me, and his care about me, and he will do with me as seemeth best to the eye of Infinite Wisdom. . . . I don't know what is in the future, but I do know that God will do as he has always hitherto done, — deal with me far more mercifully than I deserve."

So as the years sped away his hope brightened, and his Christian trust grew more firm. Still undecided in reference to his final course, he received near the close of his last term a local preacher's license, due, he said, to the entreaties of a dear college friend, Rev. J. H. Knowles, and to the encouragement of his pastor, Rev. J. M. Reid.

When the four years drew to a close, there came the saddest thing of all, the parting. June 28, a letter says, —

"Professor Lindsey has come home with his new wife. We serenaded the bride the other night, and received a nice lot of wedding-cake for our pains. I have a fine quartet here in college, and we make the streets vocal these moony nights. Oh I am sad enough to cry, sometimes, when I think that I am soon to leave, and hear no more these dear voices of my classmates and my choir. I shall never enjoy the like again, I am sure. I wonder sometimes if they think half as much of me as I do of them. It is hard for me to break the strong ties which are so closely and so thickly woven around my heart.

But so goes the world. It is our lot to be torn away from a thousand dear things, just as we learn to love them. I can't express half I feel, and it would do no good if I could."

Aug. 2, he wrote again : " I have sung for the last time with my choir. I can't keep the tears back when I think of it. These years of such associations are no small ties to bind my heart. Oh, what a world of partings this is ! It is hard

> 'to rend the heart
> With the sad thought that we must part,
> And like some low and mournful spell
> To whisper but one word, — Farewell.'

" Middletown never looked so lovely as now, when I am about to leave it."

Whether his almost constant singing, with his choir, and his quartet " on moony nights," had any effect upon his future physical condition, he sometimes questioned.

CHAPTER IV.

MARRIAGE.—TEACHING AT SANBORNTON BRIDGE.—VACATION.—NEW-YEAR'S SONG.—RETURN TO SANBORNTON BRIDGE.—VARIETY OF DUTIES.—RELIGIOUS WORK.—SICKNESS.

CALVIN graduated in the class of 1852, and married, on Aug. 10 of the same year, Eliza C. Chase of Lempster, N. H., then preceptress of New-Hampshire Conference Seminary located at Sanbornton Bridge, now Tilton.

On the 24th of that month he began teaching in the same school, under the presidency of the late lamented Dr. J. E. Latimer of Boston University. Two years he taught in that position; when Professor Latimer left, and Professor Harrington took his place, and remained thus until July, 1860.

In the year 1856 the old seminary building was demolished, and replaced by a new one.

During the erection of the new building, the places used as temporary recitation-rooms proving unsuitable for winter weather, there was an interposition of one term's vacation, which was spent in the quiet home among the Lempster hills. It was scarcely a time of rest; for, ready to welcome any call for help, Professor Harrington found opportunity to preach every Sunday for one month in Brattleborough, Vt., another month in Springfield, Mass., and other sabbaths in various pulpits in New Hampshire.

He made himself useful also by a thousand services done to cheer the hearts of aged parents; he assisted the pastor in revival efforts, and entered into various projects for the benefit of the little community where he was waiting. Money was needed to defray church expenses; and knowing it to be no easy matter for a company of less than one hundred, whose only income was what could be saved by farming on the backbone of the Old Granite State, to raise five hundred dollars a year, he became one of the workers in "getting up" a New Year's festival, and spent days and evenings in committee-meetings, rehearsals, and musical drills with the young people, for the accomplishment of their laudable purposes. Among other things he wrote for the occasion a New Year's song, and after setting it to music drilled an octet of youthful voices, whose final success in rendering it greatly delighted him.

NEW YEAR'S SONG.

Hark! the voice of midnight bells
    Waking echoes far and near;
Louder still their music swells,
    Ringing in the glad New Year.
Tower and spire take up the strain,
    Ice-bound hills send forth reply,
Watching stars shout back again
    From the chambers of the sky.

Welcome now! welcome here!
    All our voices gayly sing,
Glad New Year! Happy New Year!
    Joy and gladness bring.

Bursting forth in rival shout,
    Voice of children sweet and clear,
From the doorways peeping out,
    Hail with us their "Happy New Year!"

Thus with joy and fond embrace
  Morning dawns to greet the earth;
Thus the year with smiling face
  Heralds in his glorious birth.
Welcome now, etc.

Hark! the merry sleigh-bells play
  On the moon-lit evening air;
Laughing voices join to say,
  Banish sorrow! Banish care!
Gathered in the festive throng,
  Speak we words of social cheer,
Join we in the general song,
  Welcome to the glad New Year.
Welcome now, etc.

Returning to Sanbornton Bridge in the spring of 1857, with Rev. Lewis Howard as steward of the boarding department, they assumed together the financial responsibility of the institution, and charge of the new buildings.

During the following three years, Professor Harrington greatly enjoyed the prosperity of the seminary, the church, and the village. The number of different students during the last year was 360; the last fall term having 170 in attendance. These were years of great care and varied labor. The buildings were ample, the number of students was increasing, and every thing was calculated to awaken ambition and enthusiastic labor. The whole financial strength of the trustees had been expended in raising funds to complete the new edifice, and the school must now be run on the tuition of the students. This afforded full opportunity for exercise of ingenuity and financial ability. The ancient languages claimed the president's first attention; but he entered also whatever other gap was widest. "Necessity is the mother of invention," was an adage well illustrated in the laboratory of the new building, which afforded many amusing proofs of the effort he made to adapt all sorts of traps to the furnishing of necessary apparatus for mathematical, philosophical, and chemical purposes. These ready, the nights were taken, often until late hours, to rehearse the experiments for the coming day, lest by any means the students might discover that the success of each one was as novel and delightful to the professor as to themselves; for when he was in college there was not, as now, a department either of practical chemistry or physics.

The mineralogical cabinet was unusually respectable for a conference seminary; but in his daily walks during the term, and longer rambles in vacation, he went armed with hammer and chisel, and many a specimen from the various rich veins in New Hampshire, Vermont, Massachusetts, New York, and Canada, he added to its store. Evening lectures on all departments of science, as well as on music, reading, general culture, etc., were added to the daily routine; and class and prayer meetings claimed always one evening each per week.

His interest for his pupils reached beyond their mental needs. He longed for their spiritual good. During the last years of his stay in the seminary, he had the habit, after the school was fairly launched on a new term, of taking his roll-book, and by a private mark designating those who were not Christians; and afterwards they were, one by one, made especial subjects of his prayers and labors. He caused to be formed, among the working Christians, bands of about a dozen each, one of which he led himself. These met for a half-hour daily, and prayed for the conversion of their fellow-students. And term after term was marked by the answers to these prayers, and the adding of these especial subjects to the same bands, until they were filled to overflowing. From time to time, he baptized such converts. Near the close of one term, there were eighteen whom he thus consecrated on one sabbath to the service of the Master.

In the winter of 1858–59, during a course of lectures he was giving to the school and village community, he contracted a severe cold, which resulted in a fearful attack of pleuro-pneumonia. He was recovering slowly, when advised by his physician to go away from the seminary, that, securing rest both of mind and body, he might the more speedily regain complete health. He accordingly went to his father's at East St. Johnsbury, where, the day after his arrival, he was seized with violent relapse of the disease, so that his life was despaired of. Being told that his wife would come on the evening stage, he insisted on leaving his bed, and dressing for the occasion; and when she entered the house he stood in dress-coat and boots in the door of his room, leaning on a support, looking more like a spirit departed than a living body. It required few words to lead him back to his bed, which he did not leave again for many days. All the symptoms were so alarming, that most discouraging words went back to the seminary. On the evening of the weekly prayer-meeting, "prayer was made without ceasing, of the church, unto God for him." Rev. W. D. Cass, then a strong man in the New-Hampshire Conference, and a trustee of the seminary, prayed with such fervor and manifest faith, that those present felt that the throne of God was reached. When he arose from his knees, he said, "I have got the victory. Brother Harrington will be restored to us." The next morning — though, of course, we knew nothing of all this — we saw a decided change for the better; and from that time he steadily improved, and very rapidly. In less than a month, he was back in his place doing all his work as before.

Those eight years of labor in New Hampshire enabled him to pay off his college debt, and gave him the privilege of contributing several hundred dollars to the new school edifice, and nearly as much to the new Methodist-Episcopal Church in the village. They gave him also a home in the hearts of hundreds of young people who came under his influence, a wealth of friends, who from that time onward were continually meeting and cheering him wherever he went. They furnished him means to support his family during nine months of rest, and, after a pastorate of three months, to bring him to his next field of labor with much well-earned experience, and something less than one hundred dollars as his whole earthly store. They gave him a wealth of memories, which were always sacredly cherished, and often mentioned as causes of gratitude. The families in which we boarded there, he used to call "our homes," and their members he regarded as kindred.

CHAPTER V.

RESIGNATION. — LIFE-QUESTION. — GREAT FALLS. — CALL TO WESLEYAN. — COLLEGE-WORK. — LATIN TRANSLATIONS. — CHURCH-WORK. — "OUR COLLEGES."

IN June, 1860, he resigned his position in New-Hampshire Conference Seminary, and spent the following nine months in visiting, travelling, and general recruiting. He was a member of New-Hampshire Conference; had received the ordination of deacon in 1857 at the hands of Bishop Morris, and of elder in 1859, from Bishop Ames. He had never, however, fully settled the question whether he ought to remain a teacher, or to take work as a travelling preacher. He was not satisfied that he had a certain call to the active ministry, and feared his talents not adapted to public speaking. During these nine months of comparative leisure, he made the subject one of constant prayer and thought. And yet, when the time of Conference approached, he had no settled convictions on the matter. He said, "I will put myself in the hands of the Church, and wait further the indications of Providence."

He was appointed to High-street Church, Great Falls, N.H. He entered upon his duties with real zest, and for three months greatly enjoyed the position of pastor, and, receiving cordial support from his people, was getting quite at home in the pulpit; when an unexpected election to the chair of the Greek professorship in Wesleyan

University made him again consider the all-important question of his life-work. It was not long before it was finally settled; and, feeling now sure that this was the call of God, after amicably adjusting the matter with his people at Great Falls, he accepted the position, and removed to Middletown, Conn., in August, 1861.

Great Falls he remembered always with much pleasure as being the locality of the first home in his own hired house, the birthplace of his boy, the short pastorate where he had enjoyed for a very brief time the wealth of Christian communion and sympathy that is felt between pastor and people in one of the best of the New-England Methodist churches, and the place where a kind Providence finally wrought out for him the settlement of the great question of his life-work.

In August, 1861, he entered upon his duties as professor of Greek in Wesleyan University.

At the end of two years, after having become increasingly in love with the Greek tongue, by some process of evolution another professorship was vacated, and he was transferred from the Greek to the department of Latin, which had formerly been his favorite study. From this time he bent all his energies to perfecting his knowledge of that language; and though repeatedly compelled to add classes outside of this regular work, — as history, political economy, or Constitution, — he always did it under a mental protest, feeling that every thing of that sort was defrauding him of his opportunity to accomplish the most possible for his own department. His devotion to his college work was a religious one. No weariness of body, call of company, or any outside attraction, could induce him to leave a recitation. When told sometimes that he might be more popular with the boys if he would "give them a cut" occasionally, he would say, "I don't know how I am to keep a good conscience when I neglect any regular duty for a trivial cause." And this work was not irksome. Every year he loved it better; and even after disease had seriously depleted his strength, he went still with great pleasure to his college "sanctum," very often thanking God that he was still able to pursue his chosen calling.

Of the Latin he never tired, but from year to year his fondness for the old tongue increased. He frequently amused himself by translating from Latin to English verse. The "Methodist Quarterly Review" for October, 1870, has an article on "The Ethics of Latin Comedy," in which some score of extracts are thus rendered. Several old Latin hymns, anglicised in verse, are found among his papers. The following hymn of Peter the Venerable is a good example of the effort he enjoyed to preserve in English rhyme the poetic measure of the Latin: —

DE RESURRECTIONE DOMINI.

Pone luctum, Magdalena,
Et serena lacrymas.

Cease thy sorrow, Magdalena,
  Tearless lift thy beaming brow;
'Tis no more the feast of Simon,
  Causeless is thy weeping now.
Thousand reasons challenge gladness,
Exultation now for sadness.
                Halleluia!

Summon laughter, Magdalena,
  Let thy kindling face grow bright;
All thy suffering has departed,
  Gleams again the glowing light.

MEMORIES. 39

Lo! the world unchained through Jesus,
Triumphing, from death he frees us.
          Halleluia!

Shout for joy, O Magdalena!
  Christ has left the gloomy grave;
Finished is the sad transaction,
  Death destroyed, He comes to save.
Whom with grief thou sawest dying,
Greet with smiles, the tomb defying.
          Halleluia!

Lift thine eyes, O Magdalena!
  Lo! thy Lord before thee stands;
See! how fair the thorn-crowned forehead;
  Mark his feet, his side, his hands.
Glow his wounds with pearly whiteness,
Hallowing life with heavenly brightness.
          Halleluia!

Wake and live, O Magdalena!
  Now thy night is changed to day;
Let thy heart swell with rejoicing,
  Death's strong arm is dashed away.
Grief and lamentation spurning,
Hail thy loving joys returning.
          Halleluia!

He often used his moments of vacation recreation in reading rare old Latin authors, as his most pleasant pastime. It was interesting to him to see how they verified the words of Solomon, "There is no new thing under the sun." He would often break out with a laugh, saying, "Here it is again! such or such a modern theory is only a rehash of what this old Latin fellow wrote centuries ago." His article on Lucretius, in the "Quarterly" for January, 1876, claims that the philosophy of this ancient poet, "in its essential features, in its merits which have stood the test of centuries, and in its failures which are common to all who have followed him, is the prototype of all subsequent materialistic philosophy."

In his college life, as well as elsewhere, he made his duties to the Church of God of paramount importance. So far from finding these to require any neglect of college work, he used to say that the one aided the other. As the mental and spiritual nature complemented each other, so the labors of each mutually increased their capacity. He thought that college life, instead of tending, as he saw it often did, to lowering the standard of morality and religion, ought to be always an incentive to greater and more manifest spiritual power. He believed the design of college founders was only thus accomplished. The intensity of his feeling on this subject found expression in an article published in "The Methodist Quarterly" of October, 1879, entitled "Our Coleges," from which are the following extracts : —

"There can be no question that the original purpose of the college was mainly as an auxiliary to religion. Whatever may have been its design as a means of mental culture, the dominant one was to promote the cause of Christ. The founders of these institutions in our early history were eminently pious men. Their chief thought in their noble work was to inaugurate a powerful agency of an aggressive Christianity. No doubt they believed, what is true, that the college as a means of liberal culture, as a centre of intellectual power whose utterances should exercise an authoritative control upon the popular mind, and as a discoverer and disseminator of useful knowledge, would be such an agency in a very high sense. But that culture, intellect, and knowledge, without the vitalizing forces of religion, would realize their intent in the founding of a college, never entered their minds. Academic culture was rather the instrument of religion; a blade of cold steel, that must be tempered in the blood of Christ if it would do any real service to humanity. Education was not regarded as a Christianizing force, except in the hands of religion. Every effort to promote the one, from the common school to the college, was made on the belief that it was the outgrowth and auxiliary of the other. A large part of the funds given to found William and Mary College were given as a missionary donation, and conditioned on such an application of them. The seal of Harvard bears the motto, '*Christo et Ecclesiæ.*' The seal of Yale has the words, '*Lux et Veritas;*' and what other light and truth than that of the Holy Scriptures were in the thought of the ten clergymen who laid the foundation of that beacon on our shores? Dartmouth College began as an Indian mission. The announced purpose of the Synod of New York in founding Princeton College was, 'to supply the Church with learned and able preachers of the Word.' President Witherspoon well embodied its spirit in the words: 'Cursed be all that learning that is contrary to the cross of Christ; cursed be all that learning that is not coincident with the cross of Christ; cursed be all that learning that is not subservient to the cross of Christ.' There is not a New-England college but is the result of the religious enthusiasm of its founders as a means primarily of defending and propagating the gospel. A large number of Western colleges are missionary enterprises, designed to furnish a supply of pious and learned ministers in those new and growing regions. And the history of the very few institutions that have been founded in irreligion shows them a failure until they have passed under the controlling influence of religion. The founders of Methodist institutions were men of whom it would be sacrilege to suppose that they did not intend them to be directly, as well as indirectly, a power for Christ. They are the children of the Church, born and baptized with the hope and purpose that they should become the giants of her advancing armies, and the invincible bulwarks of her defence. . . .

"An unchristian man, or a man of doubtful religious character, much more a man of well-known sceptical opinions or an irreligious life, should have no place in a board of college instruction. Without doubt, such an opinion will be met with the charge of bigotry and illiberality. These are days in which men are exceedingly sensitive to such a charge. The glamour of liberalism charms like a Circe, and petrifies like a Gorgon. To be called narrow, is to be reckoned in conflict with the advancing tread of the ages; and to be called an adherent of the old-time faith, and pious after the Puritan fashion, is to be called narrow. Broadness is deified. Strip off the angelic garb from our Satan, and his name is Liberalism; and it becomes Christianity to do what it can to disrobe him. . . .

"We are no advocate of a dogmatic Christianity, nor of religious asceticism. The college is not a monastery. Its chief function is the culture of the intellect, through the channels of art, science, and language. But these channels will inevitably carry a moral current too. It is the solemn duty of a Christian college to see to it that its moral teaching be pure. It needs no parade of religious profession, no offensive boasts of its religious character. It should be as unostentatious as true religion always is; but it should be as firm as the hills in its principles, and well known by its fruits. . . .

"There is no goal like a Christian goal, no purpose like a Christian purpose. There is no antidote for instability, discouragement, and defeat, like Christian principle. If the atmosphere of a college is helpful for this, its students stand on the highest vantage-ground. In proportion as a college possesses this positive and leading element, will the standard of its culture rise, and the results of its mission be accomplished. . . .

"It is one of the most serious errors of the day, that the educational system of our country ought to be divested of the religious element; that this element of itself, and by itself, and in its own specific channels, is sufficient for the religious welfare of the young. Nothing is more strange than such an idea in a Christian country. Nothing but the hypocrisy of Romanism, seconded by the demagogism of politics, could have given it such currency. The very heathen have a better theory. The Constitution of Lycurgus made the morals of the Spartan child, after their standard of morality, the principal thing in their education. Philip of Macedon thanked the gods, upon the birth of Alexander, not so much that they had given him a son, as that Aristotle might be his instructor; and none like Aristotle comprehended the immortal nature of man, and strove to mould his pupils by that lofty conception. The Chinese blend religious with secular instruction, and the Persians teach their children virtue as the best of all knowledge. The Christianity of history has never dared separate religion and education. From Jesuit to Puritan, the theory and practice of education have regarded religion as the most positive and direct of its forces. It is reserved for the last half of the nineteenth century, and the most Christian of all lands, to maintain, that, in the most critical of character-forming processes and periods, it is safe to withdraw the power of a positive religious influence. As though any event of life should go on without it! And so men who would be conscience-smitten not to ask the blessing of God upon every meal, think it unimportant that the word of God and prayer should introduce the daily transactions of a school or college. It is dangerous business to make the prayers of Sunday last for the week; it is equally dangerous to offset an extra amount of religion in the family and Sunday school, against a minus quantity in the halls of secular education. . , . In the direction in which we are urging the sphere of the college, is there that active sympathy in the Church which the case demands? The college expects, and, no doubt, receives, the prayers of those Christian fathers and mothers whose sons are enjoying its privileges. Other ties than those that link the Church and the college secure them. But is the mind of the Church at all awake to the importance of the relationship? Does it half realize the power of the college for good or evil, its conservative and aggressive influence for Christ, its grasp on the Christian pulpit, its plastic power on educated mind, and, through this, on the less-thinking masses? Is not the most exclusive idea about them, in the popular mind, that they are simply intellectual gymnasia, — that if they have a good moral tone, it is well; if not, it is a necessary evil? Do they know that their highest need is a stream of prayer from the whole Church, whose constant, mighty flow shall flood them with a divine light and life? That such a need is partially felt, is seen in the establishment and observance of the day of prayer for colleges. That such a day should have been thought desirable, is high proof of their importance in many minds. But how many of the churches observe this day by any suitable exercise of worship? How many family altars and secret closets burn with sacrifice on that day? Possibly it is more widely observed than we know, but it is to be feared there is a sad neglect and a general indifference to the whole subject. If so, nothing can be more fatal to the highest interests of the Christian religion. The Church should have a jealous care for the sources of its power. . . .

"True liberalism is that which includes Christianity in all the length and breadth of Bible doctrine, and of a supernatural religious experience. The creed of modern liberalism either excludes Christianity altogether, or strips it of all supernatural authority. That creed adopted leaves the body of human learning a corpse, and nothing more. The heart and lungs of the world's thought and knowledge are revelation, and the faith it has inspired in humanity. The human mind is caged in every department of science and learning until the religion of Jesus lift the bars. Breadth of vision comes only from the heights of God. The horizon of law is infinitely broader from the summit of Sinai than from the Forum of the seven-hilled city. Political science runs mad, and leads the nations into anarchy, as soon as it leaves the council-chamber of God. Philosophy rings its dull changes through all the centuries in the narrow circles of Epicureanism, Stoicism, and Fate, until it hears the voice of the Great Teacher. Science digs in the earth like the mole, or hoots from its perch like an owl in the sunlight, until the Master opens its blind eyes. History is a labyrinth inextricable, without the golden clew of the Divine Word. And every branch of human knowledge has its only key, its richest sanction, and its proper culmination, in the religion of Christ. There is no breadth or profundity of culture without it. College education must be inspired by it, or else be soulless and dead. The college life, like the individual life, should be hid with Christ in God."

CHAPTER VI.

PASTORAL WORK.—EXTRACTS FROM DIARIES.—PRAYER.—
EXTRACT FROM SERMON.—GENERAL CONFERENCE.

DURING the year 1867, in order to secure a preacher by transfer from a Western conference, there was a space of six months during which the clerical professors in college supplied the pulpit of the Methodist Episcopal Church in Middletown, the pastoral care meanwhile devolving upon Professor Harrington. Conducting social meetings, caring for converts, visiting the sick and sorrowing, and doing other duties incident to the position, gave him a love for this people that subsequent years served only to perpetuate and strengthen. He formed church classes to include all the members, and inaugurated a children's class which still continues. Besides the meeting of students, which he always led weekly in his own recitation-room, he had, during the greater part of the time since that year, led also one of these church classes, which combined to deepen his interest and anxiety for the welfare of this church, until it became an absorbing part of his being. Oh, how, in his later years, he deplored her coldness, and prayed for her complete sanctification! Certainly, "morning, evening, and at noon," he cried unto God for the salvation of His people.

In no way can his own inner life, for a succession of

years, be better shown than by occasional extracts from his daily writings : —

April 14, 1867. — Commenced my temporary pastorate. If it may save one soul, or make any more sure my own salvation, to bear this responsibility, I ought to be willing, yea glad, to have it. Oh that the revelations of eternity may show that it has secured these things, and abundantly more!

April 21. — I judge from the details of the experiences of others, that there is an experience in the Christian life which is much more desirable than any I have yet attained. Why is it? Have I idols? Have I wrong ideas? Do I fail even yet to apprehend Christ? Oh the mystery and deception of the heart! Am I stumbling over the simplicity of faith?

May 10. — To use the grace of God, is the great skill of the Christian. It is freely furnished on the simple conditions of faith and obedience, and the amount is proportioned to our willing use of it. We cannot expect to have great spiritual power unless we *use* the grace given, and apply it to an intenser Christian life.

May 14. — In God's economy, weak things confound the mighty. Consecration may then be the measure of our strength. If we lay down our own strength, we take hold on Divine strength. In proportion as we truly say, "Not unto us," does God condescend to use our powers for his glory. But how to be still, and yet active, is the great spiritual problem.

May 26. — Rainy and disagreeable, and I must preach under disappointment. But God reigns, and orders all things; and something good somewhere will result, if not to me and here. The great question is, "How shall I, just now, do most for God and my own soul?" Teach me, O Lord, and guide me, and help me by thy power.

Sept. 7. — My mind is on the stretch for "all the fulness of God." Yesterday my heart was burdened with a leaden weight. This morning it does not seem so heavy. But I long for something that I have not, for the expulsion of unrest from my heart, for the clear light and the undoubted assurance.

Sept. 11. — It is *all* of faith, through *Jesus*. God will lead the earnest, striving soul into the ability to say, "I am crucified with Christ; nevertheless I live; yet not I, but Christ liveth in me." And in the studies of faith he will every day intensify the emphasis with which the inmost soul shall indorse it. O Jesus, at thy feet I lie.

Sept. 14. — God gives me a clearer view of the great truth that salvation in all its extent is by Jesus Christ. It is by his one offering that God has perfected them that are sanctified. Christ's holiness and righteousness and perfection belong to his believing children. In faith these are to be appropriated, and the soul cleansed.

Oct. 1. — The first frost of the season last night. It was to me a wakeful night, and in my wakeful musings it was a time of wonderful nearness to God. Oh that I might ever realize, as I did then, the reality of gospel truth! If I could, I could live better, preach better, and do much more for God. Oh, how small is my faith!

Oct. 3. — At thy feet, O Lord, my Saviour, I take my place. I am ignorant, weak, and poor; yea, I am nothing. O Lord, I am a little child; lead me and help me. In the abyss of humility I cry unto thee. Save, or I perish. And thou wilt save. They who put their trust in thee shall never be confounded. O Rock of Ages, "let me hide myself in thee."

Oct. 8. — Bless the Lord, O my soul, and forget not all his benefits. It seems to me that he *is* increasing my faith and confidence in him. Still I cry for more, wrestling with God for the gift of power, for a life that is hid with Christ in God, for prevailing power with God, for the showers of grace and the revival of his work.

Jan. 28, 1868. — Behold God, O my soul, as a Father in all thy history. Let his hand lead thy every step. Behold him as thy Saviour and Redeemer, who hath loved thee with an everlasting love. Behold him as thy unfailing Friend, more interested in thy welfare and success than thou art thyself. Behold him as all purity and holiness; and strive, oh, strive to be holy too.

March 12. — "Looking unto Jesus." To keep him ever in mind, must be the secret of all success. To appreciate his power and willingness to help us, to feel the truth that all our sufficiency is in him, is truly blessed. When we go on in forgetfulness of him, beclouded and stumbling in barrenness and coldness, we are making no progress. O Jesus, reveal thyself unto me in loving care and mercy, to make me humble and holy.

May 19. — The key to the control of the heart for God. Satan has false keys in abundance. He seems to have power to pick the most cunning lock. He has a way of getting in when we least expect or desire him. The best way is, perhaps, to set one of God's good angels to keep guard before the door, — to keep him there by careful kindness and good pay, to watch against the coming of the adversary.

June 9. — To live near to Christ, is the best way to secure immediate help when in danger through temptation. There is a peculiar power in such nearness, to strengthen us against sin. How can we stumble in the light? How can we be deceived with the light of all truth revealing the hidden snare? The sense of spiritual danger is keener, the warning is louder and quicker, when we are near to Christ.

July 2. — Communion with God is sweet and priceless. For it, it is better to sacrifice all other enjoyment, if need be. To know the favor of God resting upon us, to enjoy the exalted and glorious privilege of communion with the highest royalty in the universe, is worthy of every effort to obtain. Yet only through faith and obedience can it come to us, without money or price. Thank God for any of it!

Nov. 6. — Can the imagination more than cover the facts concerning the presence of Christ? If we strive with the spiritual senses to see, hear, feel him, and in the effort are inclined to attribute all to the imagination, and disbelieve his presence, are we not throwing away our privilege in our fear of yielding to mere imagination? Is not the truth beyond any power of conception?

Nov. 19. — When simple faith is so strong that Jesus is a delight and a joy superior to all others, the Christian life is a glorious thing. We feel as if it ought to be so oftener than it is so. Thus the perpetual struggle goes on. But "this is the victory that overcometh the world, even our faith." A strange thing is faith, yet we do not need inspiration to prove to us how mighty it is.

Dec. 27. — "In hope of the glory of God," I reach this last Sunday of the year. Full of all unworthiness, yet trusting in the merit, the infinite and glorious merit, of Christ, I still strive to do his will, and make my way to heaven. How much I find to lament in the year, and in my life, none but God knoweth. For all, I would and do repent and forsake, that I may find mercy. Have mercy, O Saviour!

May 23, 1870. — There is a place in the life of the Christian when the testimony of the Holy Spirit with the human spirit assures and satisfies the understanding of the soul's acceptance with God. This evidence is the peculiar possession of each one. It is the new name in the white stone. It is spiritually discerned.

Jan. 5, 1869. — Term begins. Oh that I may more than ever rely on God for his support and direction in the secular duties as well as the spiritual affairs of every day! Paul may plant, and Apollos water, but it is God who giveth the increase. The sanctions of Divine approval are necessary to all success, and "nothing is too hard for God."

Feb. 7. — "Have faith in God." May *I* do this? It is often a mountain barrier to faith to remember, and even faintly realize, the sinfulness and demerit in ourselves. Unworthy, unworthy, is the deep feeling, the overshadowing feeling within us, hiding all the encouragements to believe. But He who cried on the cross, "Father, forgive them," can surely in his place as our Advocate pity and forgive, and move the Father to pardon the vilest. Oh, to be a bold asker at the mercy-seat!

Feb. 24. — Repentance is the "tear in the eye of Faith." Contrition of heart is the proper attitude of all towards God. Immersed in this atmosphere of penitence, the soul sees beauty in Jesus, and in all the dealings of God toward us. As the natural atmosphere is needful to distribute and apply the rays of the sun to beautify and fructify the earth, so the atmosphere of a broken and a contrite heart is needful to a saving knowledge of the Sun of righteousness.

March 14. — It must be a day of struggle. The vague yet uncomfortable and discouraging shadows of doubt are flitting around. The dark questionings, the spiritual discontent, the self-distrust and condemnation, that result from failures and shortcomings, — these are the hosts that fight me to-day. Yet in the name of Jesus Christ I will not give up. There is hope nowhere else. There is salvation in no other. Oh for more faith and hope and love!

May 8. — Oh for more, more, *more!* So says the soul as the thought of the possibilities of the gospel comes in, and the vanities of this world become more apparent. And so the struggle goes on. Time flies. The end hastens. The garments of salvation should be as surely ours as the shroud of death will be ere long. How much the heart needs the steadying influence of grace, the ballast of divine thought, amid the storms and eddying currents that are driving us this way and that! Oh for grace!

May 17. — My forty-third birthday. Thanks be to God for the hope of spending an eternity of birthdays with my Lord, the blessed Jesus. Thanks be to him for the undeserved mercies of these mortal years. The long-suffering of God, how great it is! How should my soul magnify the Lord! What time he lets me live in the remnant of this earthly pilgrimage shall, by his grace, be spent in a more earnest effort to glorify him in my body and spirit. O Jesus! help me.

May 19. — These last few days have been marked by an especial nearness of access to God, especial sweetness in the communications of his grace. It is easier to realize the weakness and sinfulness of our hearts, when thus softened and enlightened by the Holy Spirit. Pride goes with darkness, and unbelief begets rebellion of spirit. The tenderness of heart that bows before the Lord will open the soul to see its entire dependence on Christ, and its inherent depravity.

July 25. — At Bridgeport; and the burden of preaching to a strange congregation, in a strange pulpit, is upon me. O Saviour! help me to bear this burden, or rather bear it for me. It is thy gospel. It is thy name and thy salvation. Oh, let it be precious to me, and glorious. Let my own soul be filled with fatness. Let the revelations of eternity tell of great good done in thy name. O Holy Spirit, come and inspire the unworthiest of thy mortals to speak and think for thee. So shall God be glorified, and sinners be converted unto thee.

Sept. 11. — Faith is the spiritual sense. It seems to be a combination of the natural senses in one. It brings to our spiritual apprehension the things that are unseen and eternal. It is all eye, all ear, all touch, as the spiritual sense concentrates itself. But it must be exercised in the clear light of the understanding in order to be pleasing to God. An enlightened faith is the mighty power that God gives his people. It is a glorious thing to be able to say, "I am my Lord's, and he is mine."

Oct. 23. — Another week gone. May the whirling wheels of time bring me nearer heaven as they do nearer the grave. Noiselessly the chariot of time moves on. No neighing steeds, no rushing steam, no rattling parade; but drawn by the unseen forces of God, and guided by his hand, earth bears on her millions of passengers to the eternal world. No accidents, no halting for repairs, no slackening of speed, until the parted clouds shall reveal the coming Christ.

Mr. Harrington's life was pre-eminently a life of prayer. That resolution recorded so early in his Christian experience was sacredly kept. He never left his room in the morning, no matter how cold the air, no matter how late the hour, no matter what cares were awaiting, without first falling on his knees, and spending many minutes in secret communion with his God. This was followed regularly by taking his Bible, as soon as he reached the parlor, and studying carefully a portion of the sacred book. Immediately after breakfast was our season at the family altar, when he armed himself anew for the day's warfare. We can never forget the pathos and unction with which he sang those morning songs of Zion, or the fervency of his prayers as he daily committed us all to the especial care of our Heavenly Father, or the look of trust on his face as he hurried away to morning prayers at college chapel, a service he never lost without feeling really afflicted thereby. Neither were all his prayers in the morning; nor did the evening altar or the night vespers comprise them: but he understood what it meant to "pray without ceasing," to "pray everywhere." In a description of a pedestrian tour from Rome to Albano, he wrote: "Strolled round the lake by the upper gallery. Beautiful. *Multo bello.* It was a good place to pray under an evergreen oak."

He had great confidence in the prayers of others. In a letter to his sister he wrote: "There is nothing more comforting than to know that we are resting on the prayers and sympathies of friends, and I believe they have a prevailing efficacy above." From one of his sermons we have this extract: "We may never know, this side of eternity, how far we are indebted to the efforts of others for our present gracious condition, whatever it be; but, without doubt, the debt is immense. The word of God recognizes such efforts as an important element in Christian culture, both for the Church and the individual. 'Pray for the peace of Jerusalem,' wrote the inspired Psalmist, centuries ago. That exhortation, heeded by the Church, has many a time rebuilt her ruined walls, or strengthened her tottering towers. The fulfilment of the apostle's command, 'Pray one for another,' has doubtless wrought, a thousand times, the establishment of the wavering, or the recovery of the erring. How touching the prayer of Moses for Israel, 'If thou wilt forgive their sin — and if not, blot me, I pray thee, out of thy book;' and who can tell its influence in averting destruction? Was it not the prayer of Abraham that delivered righteous Lot from the fiery overthrow of Sodom? Did not the servant of the centurion live because of his friendly intercession? and was not the ruler's daughter raised to life in answer to the ruler's request? These Bible illustrations are but the specimens of myriad instances of the results of human efforts in behalf of others. Eternity will make many strange revelations. It will be found then that national deliverance, social revolutions, and the life-career of individuals, have hinged upon the superhuman help which God has furnished just when needed, in answer to the exertions of others. Thousands will have to say, in the fruition of glory, 'By the grace of God, through a mother's prayers, I am what I am.' Thousands are in the midst of gracious surroundings, that mould their lives, all unconscious that they are the living stream of generations, whose silent flow begins far back in the springs of some pious struggle for the welfare of posterity. This man's missionary life-work, that man's career of usefulness, another's narrow escape from the drunkard's doom, the rescue from especial sinful tendencies, the opportunities for culture, the barrier that has changed the course of life, the ray of hope that has saved from despair, the cloud of adversity that has tempered the too blinding radiance of prosperity, the stroke of sorrow which, by the divine surgery, arrests the progress of fatal disease, — these things, and thousands more that have made us what we are, we shall thankfully say hereafter, are the gracious fruit of superhuman help given through special pleas in our behalf. Everywhere the finger of man touches us; and, in the lifting of the curtain of divine mystery, we shall see that it is the finger of God."

As the years passed on, labors increased. From a letter written to his brother in January, 1872, is the following : —

"The work of life sometimes seems burdensome. Every hour is crowded with duties, until I hardly know which way to turn. It is a lesson which I find hard to learn, to let cares and responsibilities sit easy on my heart and mind, and so avoid the wear and tear in some degree. But when I can rise to the height of trying to do all things 'heartily as unto the Lord, and not as unto men,' it is easier and happier. But how hard it is, sometimes, to put away worldly motives and ambitions, to discard selfishness, and work for God and humanity ! How good is the Lord to bear with our infirmities and failures, and let us try again ! But I thank God I see a little progress, and find a little comfort, in the struggle to overcome the world, the flesh, and the Devil.

"I am glad you enjoyed your visit with us. I feel, as you do, more and more enjoyment in the meeting of friends as I grow older, and their love is more and more precious to me. Life would be a dreary thing, were it not for some few to love us and appreciate us. The circle must be narrow in this world, but I go for making the most of it. It is a little while we stay here, but we can use the blessings of life better as we learn their value more. I think we can keep each other a little nearer the throne of mercy than ever, when we put up our morning and evening and our closet prayers. It will soon be over : let us be faithful."

In the spring of 1872 Mr. Harrington was elected a delegate to the Methodist General Conference held in

Brooklyn. Some of the incidents and thoughts the session occasioned are found in his diary: —

April 30. — To-day I start for Brooklyn. I leave my dear ones in the care of God. I commit my ways unto the Lord, and pray for wisdom and grace. In the untried experiences of the next few weeks I shall need to walk with God. May my soul come out of the trial pure!

May 1. — The day, with its interests and responsibilities, has come. Once more I pray for grace and wisdom from on high. Once more I record my gratitude to God for mercies past. Let all my added life be the Lord's. Bless the dear ones at home.

May 2. — Amid all the advantages of this contact with men, may I have the infinitely better one of communion with God. To make the most of the first, I shall need the second. Oh for clear and uninterrupted intercourse with him!

May 11. — The end of the week is at hand, — a week of interest and profit, I trust. Things do not go altogether as I desire; but the Lord is Governor, and will overrule all things to his honor and glory. Oh for the spirit of the Master!

May 21. — To-day is set for the election of bishops. It will be very hard for all to say, "In honor preferring one another." May the Lord help me to feel so, and, with an eye single to his glory, to cast my vote for the men who are approved of God.

The scramble of partisans is offensive. Can God overrule and mercifully bring good out of evil? These elections are probably necessary, but I do wish the worldliness of the thing could be eliminated. Lord, help me to seek honor of thee.

June 4. — The last day of General Conference. The instruction, the privileges, the relief from routine duties which it has given me, will be a grateful memory with me for a long time, I think. The end of all things comes. May I be ready for *the* end!

June 5. — Home again, thank God! And he has blessed my going out and my coming in. Praise to his holy name. So, in resuming the labors and duties of my calling, I expect the rich blessing of God still. Let me trust and love him with all my heart.

One morning during the session of the Conference, as some question of vital importance to the Church was being discussed, to which Mr. Harrington was listening with intense interest, careful not to lose one word that might be of advantage in forming a just opinion, a messenger called him to the lobby. There he found awaiting him one of the younger members of his own Conference, who unceremoniously commenced parading arguments upon the topic then under discussion, and finally said, "You know, brother Harrington, the views of our Conference in this matter, and I suppose you understand that in voting you are expected to carry out the wishes of your constituents." Those who remember brother Harrington's utter contempt of every thing like political wire-working may easily imagine his lips growing a little thinner, his eye a little brighter, and his face a little paler, as he replied in measured tones, "I understand no such thing: I understand that I am to use my own best judgment, and to be governed by my own conscience;" and turning on his heel, he hastened back to his seat on the Conference floor.

At this conference he was made one of the Committee on Church Extension. He received the appointment with gratitude that he was permitted thus to work with the Church, to promote its greater power. His interest in that cause intensified during those four years of service, and continued ever afterward; leading him, the last time he attended his conference at Manchester, N.H., in 1884, to answer one of Chaplain McCabe's irresistible appeals with two hundred and fifty dollars to build one of his "two-a-day" churches.

CHAPTER VII.

EUROPEAN TOUR.—LETTERS, AND EXTRACTS FROM DIARIES.

HE was naturally fond of travel. He had an almost morbid love for sight-seeing. Added to these, a desire to gain all facilities for advantage in the work of his department gave him an increasing anxiety to spend some time in Europe, especially among old Roman scenes. In the spring of 1873 he determined to devote the summer vacation to that purpose. This necessitated separating from his family, as the purse was too short to provide for three, and to leave the boy of twelve without parental restraint and care was a thing not to be thought of. The struggle this caused was repeated three days before the time for sailing, when the trustees kindly proposed to allow him one term of absence, making the "good-bys" to be said for six months instead of three. The offer was gratefully accepted; and in company with his pastor Rev. J. E. Breckenridge, Prof. R. G. Hibbard of the university, and Rev. A. Hill of the New-York East Conference, he sailed from New York on June 28. The following letter from the home of his brother-in-law in New York shows his thoughts at the time: —

"SATURDAY MORNING, JUNE 28,
In Lucius's back parlor.

"That date up there has a fruitful meaning. It comprehends more than I have time or power to express. It is the realization of hope and the dawn of fear; a fulfilment and a promise; a joy outward to which I hold my hands in welcome, and a grief inward from which I shrink; a line of separation that cuts me in two, — or *three*, — and leaves my better parts behind; a threshold of departure for scenes and experiences in themselves desired, but covered, as every thing earthly is, with regrets. But how good God is! I don't know that I ever felt safer for you and myself than now. I have just read the chapter in John that you will read this morning, and a chapter in sister Loveland's book about the blessed brotherhood of Christ; and I know that if we abide in him, he will abide in us."

"I had a dull, sleepy ride to this city of noise and bustle. My head was hung on a pivot, and wabbled round strangely under the blind hand of Somnus. He twisted and turned it as he would, for all I could do. But in due time I arrived at this house, to find the people at tea, and down I went to sit at my place among them. . . . I have not yet thought of any thing omitted in regard to matters at home. Act your discretion about any thing that needs doing about the premises that has been overlooked. Shut the cellar-windows when you go away. Put the padlock on the barn-door. Have the large gate shut and barred, etc., etc., etc. . . .

"On the 'Adriatic,' in our room. Well. Lucius by my side. Now, good-by, and God bless you."

July 2, he wrote from the steamship "Adriatic:" —

"We are on the Banks. We are in a bank of fog. This is the fifth day out, and yet to-day, at noon, we had run eight hundred and ninety-two miles. All day yesterday and all night the fog-whistle has sounded its deafening yells every two minutes. The fog is so dense, that the forward watch cannot see much more than the ship's length. But there he stands, all day and all night, peering out into the mist and darkness; and ever and anon in the night, as the bell tolls the hour, his 'All's well' gives a very cheering sense of security. The boatswain's piping whistle calling the hands to man the ropes, the chorus of their voices as they sing the refrain, and pull the huge tackling of boom and sail, the officers pacing their beat on the bridge, the helmsman forever at the wheel, the steady rumbling of the engine that never stops to breathe or rest, the precision and order with which every movement goes on, — all tell of safety, and assure us that with the Father's good blessing we shall soon reach our haven. . . .

"All day Monday, the steamer 'Rhine,' that left about two hours before us, kept off our starboard bow in plain sight, neither gaining nor losing much. Since then the fog has hidden her. On the same day, the 'Cuba,' of the Cunard Line, passed us in fine style, within hailing distance. A sailing ship appears now and then. On this desert deep, it is an event to see an occasional fellow-traveller. The solemn voice of the ocean teaches brotherhood and fellowship, and makes friends of strangers. It makes all who rest upon its broad catholic bosom forget for the time their individuality, and consent to be children of one household. . . . We are hardly beyond the influence of the land we have left yet; and as for the beloved ones who tread it, we feel their influence some, too. We are paying out a strong cable every inch we make, and have no fear that storm or accident or any thing else can interrupt the daily communication along the wires of the heart. . . .

"It is getting a little monotonous. Sailing, sailing all the day. We promenade the long deck, gaze off into the fog, gather in knots and talk, go down to breakfast, to lunch, to dinner, read books, plan routes, try to be jolly, wonder who such a one is, or such a one, play chess now and then. Karl comes up before the mind with some distinctness. And thus in various ways the time goes on, and we wish ourselves at Cork. Shall I be a Paddy then, an' sure? . . . It was hot enough the day we left port. A very dark, heavy thunder-cloud came up in the north, and appeared in full majesty sweeping down the Hudson, just as we fired our parting gun. The lightnings were very vivid, and the thunder rolled heavily behind us. On came the storm, as we steamed away from it; down the bay and along the shores of green, past the harbor forts, and the forests of masts. The rain did not catch us, but the whole sweep of the black clouds, and the falling rain, and the threads of lightning, were in full view behind. Half a mile or more away from the Battery, with its little patch of green forest, flanked by an acre of bare masts, I saw the whole of that little area on the edge of the city blaze at once into sunlight. There it lay, a spot of brightness, that the sun through a cloud-rift had kissed into glory. The black thunder-head towered behind it, and the waves were its fringe before it. Thus the smile of my Father seemed to bless my going forth from native land, and all my heart holds dear on earth. Under that smile I hope to keep, and I take it as a pledge that in his good time I shall come again to enjoy the blessings of the past."

His journal during the whole of his absence was kept without a day's interruption, giving quite a full account of all the sights and scenes, incidents and accidents, that filled up the days and months of absence, spiced occasionally with bits of humor, of moralizings, and heart-yearnings. A few extracts may give a general idea of his life during the time: —

July 7. — From the port window of my berth, this morning, my eyes opened upon the *land*. It was a bold, rocky coast, and so continues. Fastness Light lay on the right of our course, and Cape Clear on our left, just visible in the distance, as I went on deck. The wind was blowing a stiff breeze, and the weather was thick and unpleasant. But a little bright patch of sunshine glistened on the waters, as if to welcome us with a smile to a foreign land. I don't wonder that Columbus fell prostrate upon the earth, and kissed it, when he landed after his perilous voyage of discovery. Any land seems good enough to kiss after eight days' confinement on shipboard. The Lord be praised! Thanks to him who has saved us from the perils of the deep!

Aug. 3. — It is a new experience to be exiled from home, country, and friends. I realize something of what it must be to be expatriated. To a warm heart, profoundly affected with the influences of domestic life, and depending largely upon the sympathy of loved ones for daily happiness, the punishment must be severe. Yet if country only is lost, the inscription that the regicide Ludlow chose and placed upon his house at Vevay, " *Omne solum forti patria,*" may cheerfully and proudly be assumed; for with a clear conscience, and a few hearts that love us, we can live and die contented anywhere. The thought that exile from God and the good, from friends and kindred, is to be the fate of the finally impenitent, impresses me more than ever before. To be banished from the presence of God and the glory of his power, must be sufficiently terrible. To long for the loving presence and sympathy of the pure and holy, will be enough without the forced association of the bad. O Father! save me from such a doom. Help me to hate sin with a perfect hatred. . . . How thankful ought I to be for the goodness and mercy of God to unworthy me! How real is the comfort wherewith I am comforted in Christ Jesus! I will strive to dwell in the "secret place of the Most High," that I may "abide under the shadow of the Almighty."

Aug. 8. — Here, on the wooden step of a Swiss barn, at Inden, I write, while the horses eat their "sagina" bread. We have eaten our bread and milk and honey, and a good meal it was. . . . It has been a climb all the way by the zigzag steep up from the valley of the Rhone. We arrived at Leuker-bad about half-past two P.M. Thence to Schwarenbach over the Gemmi Pass. It was a jaunt. But the scenery is sublime. As we at last emerged from the rocky depths to find "Alps on Alps arise" about us, and touched the path which, though 7,553 feet above the sea, is still flanked by lofty mountains and precipices on either hand; as we looked upon the mountain, lake, and glacier, and snow, — my soul went out in praise to Him who reared the mountains, and magnified in song the love of the glorious Redeemer. "Oh, for this love let rocks and hills," etc.

Aug. 10. — The twentieth anniversary of our wedding-day. How I would love to sit among my dear ones to-day in Lempster! How has God blessed me in all these years of wedded life! . . . What shall I render unto him for all his benefits? "Unto thee do I commit my spirit, for thou hast redeemed me, Lord God of truth." . . .

The Jungfrau lighted up her silver horn to-night. A cloud wrapped her feet, and golden sunlight played about her head. I thought of the Mount of God, and of the throne of glory on which the Judge shall sit at his second coming. The cloud cut it off from the earth, and it hung in the horizon as a huge mountain of light resting on the unseen hand of God.

Aug. 13. — At Lucerne, where we arrived in season for the last boat to Righi. Met on the wharf Rev. J. P. Taylor and wife. How pleasant to meet friends so! Is it a type of what it will be to greet friends on the other shore?

Aug. 16. — We have left Switzerland. The beautiful waters of Lake Maggiore received us after a two-hours' ride from Bellinzona. A poor dingy boat, in ill keeping with the green waters and the verdant shores, became our conveyance to Verona. The hills and mountains softened and rounded their outline, and towered in a benign grandeur, as if a soothing hand had been laid upon them. Alpine ruggedness, the sharp, cold fingers of her needle-peaks, the glitter of her snowy horns, her slumbering glaciers that pillow their heads in the clouds and uncover their feet in the green valleys, the thunder of the avalanche, the roar and rush of the mountain torrent, are all gone; and dreamy, sunny, soft, luxuriant, delicate Italia is here. The ripple of green waters that change again to blue, the vine, the olive, the fig, that dip their shadows in the lake, the mountains bending their green brows above, the islands that float like gardens of Paradise, — who can help thanking Him who made the soul of man to be delighted with beauty, and made such a world of beauty to satisfy and bless the eye?

Aug. 17. — [In Milan.] Our morning church-going has been to the cathedral. No doubt curiosity was a large element in our motive. How far it is sinful, I do not know. But I try to worship among these who, many of them, do so sincerely. It was high mass, so they said. There was a procession of women, men, and boys, with long candles, and a canopy, and a banner, and gilded crosses, chanting and responding; boys swinging censers that filled the aisles with smoke. There were bowings and genuflections, and singing and reading and preaching; all alike hollow and unmeaning to me, save as my soul caught a little of the inspiration of praise in the waves of music from voice and organ, as they swelled among the arches and aisles and pillars of the massive edifice, and a little of the ardor of the preacher in his earnest manner, and a little of the general spirit of devotion that always pervades a worshipping assembly.

The rich and the poor, citizen and soldier, silks and rags, all are here with equal rights in the most magnificent church edifice in the world, in common worship. Let Protestants learn a lesson.

A little boy, too small to reach or even climb to the vessel that contained the holy water and the box for the poor, attracted attention by his persistent endeavors to do both. He at last succeeded, through the kindness of a by-stander. All alone the little fellow struggled. How thoroughly the child-mind is permeated by the lessons it learns with eye and ear!

Aug. 30. — Early this morning I had my first experience in sickness on my journey. The attack was severe, so much so that I was glad to send for a physician, and had some fear that the cholera had seized me. To-day has been a hard day bodily, and the regret that my sickness interrupts brother Breckenridge's most cherished plan of seeing Rome is very great. He is very kind and self-sacrificing. May the Lord reward him!

Aug. 31. — This is one of the trial days of my journey. Providence seems to hedge up the way of our going to Rome together. The time hastens when I must pursue my journey entirely alone, when my company and my enjoyment must be confined to the novelty and interest of new scenes and travels. I expect hours of loneliness, and must, with all the joy of realizing my hopes of seeing Italy and Rome, take the bitter with the sweet. I am under the little cloud of bodily suffering, yet strong is the confidence that "he that dwelleth in the secret place of the Most High shall abide under the shadow of the Almighty." I shall yet praise Him who is the health of my countenance.

Sept. 1. — So the hot months of July and August have passed away. In perils by land and sea, God has been with me to protect and save. Through the threatened illness of the last two days he has brought me, so that, in good hope of full recovery, I set out for Milan. Thanks be to God and our ever-blessed Redeemer.

Sept. 7. — Sunday in Florence. An attempt to attend church at the American Chapel this morning failed, there being no service. So the stimulus of social worship, and of the living voice in the utterance of religious truth, is wanting. Yet my heart has rejoiced in God, and felt the kindlings of his love. I long to know better the meaning of that saying of Christ, "If any man love me he will keep my words, and my Father will love him, and we will come and take up our abode with him." That poor, unworthy man should thus be the abode of God, — how can it be? But, Lord, I claim the promise. O heavenly Guest, come in! Thou shalt have all this tenement. Thou shalt command all my feeble service. The temple shall be purified for thee, and sanctified by thee. In God will I trust, and he shall be "my help and my shield."

Sept. 10. — The Uffizi Gallery occupied me till two o'clock. I cannot pronounce upon it yet. Then the *battistero* with its brazen doors. An episode was a Catholic child-baptism by pouring. All the infants of the city are baptized here. Then I climbed to the cross on the brazen doors of the Cathedral. What a thrill came over me as I threw my arm about it, and thought, "I am at the foot of the cross"! Lord, let me abide there.

Sept. 11. — The Uffizi has a long throat from the Pitti entrance; and its sweetness kept me a good two hours to-day, before I fell into the purer sweets of the "Tribuna." I struggled out of this, however, and made my way to the Academy. How tame the modern pictures there seem! yet some of them are good. But the large room of the old masters there has gold and gems. Then the beautiful mazes of the Boboli Gardens swallowed me up, until I sighed for the clew to escape from the enchantment.

Sept. 12. — . . . The Laurenziana Biblioteca interested me much with its old manuscript copies of Virgil and Homer, and other ancient books of the ninth and twelfth centuries. How I would love to spend months in that library!

Sept. 13. — I have been half drowned, also, to-day in the Strozzi, Uffizi, and Pitti galleries. The creations of the masters in painting begin to move me. It seemed to me to-day, as I stood before the portraits of the painters, that in them I could see what their peculiar characteristics as artists would be. The delicacy and tenderness of Raphael's face, the intellectuality, energy, and soul in Leonardo de Vinci, the free, easy dignity of Rubens, are qualities which, I fancy, are transferred to their pictures. Do not a man's soul and character appear in his face? So ends a most enjoyable week. And yet the treasures of Florentine art are only glanced at. Thanks to my heavenly Father for all the week has brought of mercy and blessing.

Sept. 14. — I have walked and revelled to-day in the galleries of God. The chambers of the soul are spacious, and God has hung there many a portrait and many a glorious picture. They reveal all the phases of the soul's history, all the reality of its present condition, all the possibilities and hopes and glories of its redeemed state. We do not like to visit these halls. We close the shutters and let fall the curtains, lest our eyes should fall upon some of these paintings. For we ourselves have been the artists, and the portraits and the scenes are too faithful transcripts of ourselves and of our history. We tremble lest in some spiritual parallel to Titian's Medusa with its writhing serpents, to Guido's Peter in tears over his denial of Christ, to Leonardo's Judas with his dark brow of treachery, to the cruel beauty of Herodias' daughter with the bloody head of John, to the lustful nakedness of Pontormo's Venus, we should see our own features of passion and corruption and alienation from God.

But it need not be so. We may find ourselves mingling joyously with the shepherds that have hastened to the manger, or with the Magi that bring precious gifts to the infant Christ. We may find ourselves bending in as rapt joy and adoration over the Babe as Correggio's Madonna. We may clasp the cross on which the Saviour hangs, with as much sorrow and devotion as Guido's or Perugino's Magdalen. We may gaze with as much holy confidence into the face of the Saviour on the judgment throne, as those in Raphael's painting who have just heard the words, "Come, ye blessed of my Father." And everywhere as we walk through these wonderful halls of the spirit, we may *feel* that our Companion is by our side ; and while we gaze with tears upon all the sinful transcripts of ourselves, and the pictures of our follies, he turns us gently to the babe of Bethlehem, the cross of Calvary, and the glories of Paradise. O wonderful Christ! I will love thee more. Oh, let all the pictures that shall still be hung in the chambers of the soul breathe the inspiration of thy touch in every line.

Sept. 17. — (At Rome.)   Here I am.   A pleasant ride has brought me here unmarred by accident. I have already walked on the Corso, and listened to the band in the Piazza Colonna. Let me be duly thankful for all the mercies and favors of God. And may my stay here be blessed of him in every sense.

Sept. 20. — . . . I have looked also upon the Capitoline Hill, and the Forum with its ruins. The first glance gives me the impression that it is a very small place for so much history, and yet that it was the focus for the magnificence and splendor of antiquity. What a sorrowful sight! What a wreck the grandeur of imperial Rome has become! Like the cinders and ashes in the Etruscan urns, the relics of the Eternal City are uncovered in all their nothingness to the gaze of the living generations, that go slowly past with a sigh and an exclamation, and think of them no more. A few trinkets and some jewels are found in those ancient rooms; but they are buried in the ashes, or lie among the shapeless ruins. So a few ornaments and a few shapeless bones are all that this grave of the world's great mistress shows, to enable the looker-on to tell how noble and beautiful she was. Yet the mammoth scale of the relics is significant. I must contemplate it more.

The Mamertine Prison I have seen too. Would that my eyes were keen enough to read the history on its walls! What a palimpsest of stone, if all the sighs it has heard had registered themselves, if its tears had written their language, if its groans had translated themselves on its dark walls! Was Paul here, and Peter? Did I look upon the same walls, and upon the stony pillar where they were chained? Was I among the shades of the Catilinian conspirators, who suffered death here for their crimes? Did I hear the happy shouts of the jailers of the apostles, as they were baptized into the faith of the blessed Christ? Did I touch the same walls that apostolic hands have touched, and, in the narrow limits of so sacred a prison, feel the spirit breath of those who stood there so long? It did not require great fancy to live for a few moments with the Gentile apostle.

Sept. 23. — From the campanile of the Capitol a most splendid view rewarded the ascent. Oh, if one could summon the shades of the past to move around him, and the crumbling structures of the centuries gone, to start into the splendor of their former magnificence! But the Rome of to-day is a mosaic of life and death, of sepulchres and monuments and ruins blending with rising palaces and the varied forms of busy life; a dark picture of sorrow.

Sept. 28. — One misses home and the dear ones there more on Sunday than any other day. That is the day when not only the ordinary benefits and joys of home-life are better appreciated, but the hallowing influences of religion are added. A pause in the whirl and movement of the week makes real the difference between rest and motion. The tension of the domestic chords that have been benumbed by the excitement of business is felt when all is still. And then the touches of Christian faith and hope and love kindle new fires, and forge new bonds that blend with and strengthen the ties of nature.

Rome has little of religious attraction for me. Rich as it is in other treasures, the treasures of art and antiquity, it is barren enough in practical and vital religion. Fountain-head, as it claims to be, of the world's Christianity, and boasting of its wealth of saintly bones and holy relics and martyr-blood, it is a dry-spring of pure faith, and poor as poverty in living bone and sinew and blood. It is clinging to the corpse of a dead past, hovering over sepulchres and catacombs, climbing holy staircases, dipping holy water, kissing holy footprints and brazen toes, following the shadowy ghost of tradition, and ever mumbling something that neither it nor the nations understand.

Oct. 7. — The mausoleum of Hadrian. What changes has the dismantled old pile seen? A tomb for the dead, a prison for the living, a refuge for the Popes, a fortress for the terror of his subjects, and now the king's.

Oct. 13. — At Naples. In company with Dr. G. M. Steele, I left Rome. The route hither is along the dreary summits of the Apennines, and through a poor and poorly cultivated country, over ground full of classic and historic interest. Vesuvius showed itself with veiled head, as we approached the city, and its furrowed sides looked as we might expect they would after the fiery ploughshare has been so often driven through them.

Oct. 14. — I have just returned from Vesuvius. At 7.30 this morning Dr. Steele and I took a *fiacre* for Resina, the place where the ascent is commenced from the Naples side. The horse was largely bones, the driver antiquated, the cab rickety. The scenery along the street was an astonishing, amusing, and picturesque combination of ragged people; dingy boxes and baskets; walking caryatides supporting huge vessels of water or baskets of vegetables on their heads; sorry donkeys, the motive-power for big panniers that covered all but ears and tail; piles of tempting grapes, pomegranates, figs, and oranges, big kettles of boiled walnuts, fish, johnny-cake; go-carts covered with from twelve to twenty human beings, and drawn by one poor animal; and a hurly-burly of craftsmen and tradesmen, all intent upon the business of the day.

Dr. Steele's gray led the way, and my humble black followed meekly on from the station at Resina. After a little we came upon the lava-fields, the most noticeable being those of 1858, 1861, and 1872. The shapes of the black masses are of every fantastic variety. It was as a battle-field, as the folded leaves of a book, as the paws of lions, the backs of alligators or tortoises, as the twisted gnarled roots of trees, and a hundred other things. Arrived at the cone, we were beset by offers of help. But we meant to help ourselves. Dr. Steele, contrary to his usual disposition, as all his friends know, was inclined to be facetious at their expense; at which I nearly lost my balance with laughter, and almost fell backwards down the steep. They finally saw the but of an American joke, and ceased to pester us.

At the crater we smelt a great deal of sulphur, gathered specimens, thrust our sticks into the glowing lava until they took fire, rolled stones into the maw of the crater, walked round the rim, speculated upon the probabilities of descending inside, ate roasted eggs hot from Tartarus, and reflected much on the scientific questions that the situation suggested. The doctor was curious to know the effect of turning the Mississippi River into the mouth of the crater. The smoke, heavily charged with sulphurous fumes, varied, and gave us varying views.

The descent was easy, fully establishing the accuracy of Virgil's statement. What it took us an hour to do in ascending, the doctor accomplished in seven minutes, and I in a little more. Judging by the vast leaps we made, and admitting Darwinianism, our ancestors must have been kangaroos.

The views of the wonderful Bay of Naples, and the surrounding country, are most lovely. The cities sleeping on the beach and in the country, the bay, Sorrento, Capri, Proscini, — all make the view from Vesuvius one of unparalleled beauty and interest.

Oct. 18. — The Blue Grotto, on the island of Capri, is entirely unique. We had to get below the sides of the boat to enter the low aperture with safety. A strong gust of wind blew outward from the cave, and the waves sometimes almost closed the entrance. Once in, every thing was bathed in a peculiar bluish, silvery light. It had a kind of phosphorescent play on the ceiling and sides of the cave, and gave the water a most beautiful appearance. The oars seemed to dip in transparent silver, and the body of a swimmer took the same color. The refraction of the light colored and permeated every thing.

It might illustrate spiritual truth. The waters of the bay are just as blue outside of the grotto as within, but they give no color to the boats or men they bear upon their bosom. It is only when, through the low, narrow entrance, they enter into the rock, that they are covered and transformed by the waves that bear them, and the light that surrounds them. It is the same light, and they are the same waves; but the general effect is not visible when out on the open sea, under the sky. So of Christian truth. It has no transforming power when men only come under its general influence. It is only when, bowing low in humble contrition, they suffer themselves to be carried through the narrow door into the living Rock, that they are bathed and permeated with the heavenly light. It is only while they dwell there, that they abide under the shadow of the Almighty. Even the shadow of the Almighty is light unapproachable.

Oct. 19. — Sunday has been without the interest of those external helps that native land and tongue give to promote its legitimate enjoyment. The value of social worship and Christian sympathy, like all other blessings, is realized when we are deprived of them. . . . I am alone with my thoughts and with my God. But the ceaseless roar of passing vehicles, the clatter of hoofs on the pavements, and the general bedlam of the street, do not favor quiet meditation. . . . How wise the command that neither man nor beast should work, that the day be kept holy, that our thoughts should not be our own, but God's! For all these are essential to man's highest welfare on the Lord's Day. Those who make it a day of recreation and pleasure, under the pretext that it is only a day of rest from labor, know nothing of its ultimate design to bring man nearer to God. To make no effort to hallow the sabbath, is to rob it of the marrow of its sweetness, and to ignore one of the wisest provisions of God to fit man for a holy eternity.

The squalid, dirty poor hunt their scanty food, in their week-day rags or nakedness; the working classes don their best, and seek some form of pleasure, or lounge in the public square; the wealthy expect as much of their domestics and servants as on any other day, sleep away their mornings, dress in their finery for the drawing-room, and ride in their splendid equipages in the cool of the day; tradesmen open or close their shops, as they prefer profit or pleasure. The Romish clergy have no higher idea of a holy sabbath than the formal observance of established ceremonials, and never rebuke the violation of it; and so Naples has no real sabbath day, more than if the commandment had never been given. And the same is true of Christian Continental Europe. What a sad comment on the power of a catholic Christianity in the eighteen centuries of its history, or rather, on its false teaching and corrupt practices, its devitalized formality and soulless shell! How sad will be the day when laxity of principle, and insidious excuses, and the influence of foreign example, shall introduce such a sabbath into America!

Oct. 26. — I wish I could conceive and realize better the scenes and facts of history. There must be some power of abstraction, — some way of transforming one's self into the past, — such that the words of the men who have spoken with wisdom and authority shall be living words. If I could catch the inspiration of Paul! If the ages would melt away, the present vanish, the past emerge from the darkness and desolation and death that shroud it! How I would love to stand by Paul's side, and look over his shoulder as he writes some of those words that the world calls inspired, and fathom the depths of his heart under the touch of the divine breath, as, mysteriously impelled, he pens the immortal words! Oh, how I would love to stand under the cross where Jesus died, and catch that look, and hear those words! How I wish I could stand under that cloud on the heights of Bethany, and see the ascending Lord! Oh for a quickening of the eye and ear and touch of faith, since faith is the substance now, and has been made the evidence of things not seen!

Nov. 1. — I have been taking farewell looks at the most interesting things in Rome. There is a sense of sadness in the thought, "I shall see them no more." As one goes to say last adieus and shake hands on parting with old friends, so I have done with the ruins and monuments of this ancient city. My route has been to S. Maria Maggiore, which is always new; S. Prasseda, with its pillar to which Christ was fastened to be scourged, its slab for a couch to S. Prasseda, its blood of the martyrs, and its relics; the ruins of aqueducts and water-towers, utilized for the most varied purposes; the fine old ruin of Minerva Medica, well-preserved and impressive; S. Croce, with its traditional true cross of S. Helena; S. Giovanni, the Pope's own; the baptismal font of Constantine; the Scala Santa, and its climbing devotees; the Coliseum, grander and more impressive than any other Roman ruin; the Via Appia, thence to the Forum, with all its wealth of memories; the Forum, too comprehensive to be appreciated; the Mamertine Prison, with its wonderful walls; and all the atmosphere of the Capitoline, which is heavy with history. And now, Saturday night, I go to rest for the holy day.

Nov. 16. — This morning, I went before breakfast to St. Michael's Church to hear the music. It was classical and good, as music, but as worship I did not feel inspired by it. There is a tendency in the concord of sweet sounds to inspire a spirit of worship in souls that love music. But mere music is hollow. One must catch the soul of the composer if his music have soul, and that must be full of worship; or else the listener must supply for himself the lack, by uniting it with poetry or sentiment that helps to body it, so to speak, into definite spiritual form. I could not do that this morning, and came home unfed.

I have visited the cemetery at Munich, — the old and the new. I noticed the graves of Frauenhofer, Gaertner, Schwanthaler, and some others whose names I recognized as eminent in the world. They lie as low as the poor and the unknown, and Death has passed his levelling hand on all alike. . . .

There is a wreath of green and flowers on almost every tomb. It seems to be a German custom, thus to deck the graves of the dead. It is well to remember those that are gone, by honoring the place where they sleep: yet there is a higher honor and a sweeter communion through the channels of the memory. It requires another kind of effort to reach the spirits of those we have loved on earth; but why should we materialize all our thoughts of them in marbles, or wreaths of evergreen, or scattered flowers, often strewn upon the dust? Why not rather shut ourselves in with them in the solemn stillness of the soul, and visit a remembered life, instead of the ashes of the sepulchre?

Dec. 1. — This has been a bright day of sunshine. The shops displayed their tempting contents as I passed, but I could not buy. The Tower of St. Jacques did not pay for the ascent. The smoke had gathered, and settled over the city. A walk along the quays was aggravating, because I could not buy the books that looked at me so longingly. I had to put the dear beggars off, — hard as it was. Napoleon's tomb was the next point. It is probably the most exquisite and beautiful in the world. The hero lies no more "on a lone barren isle." But he lies in dust, and there is only a name left, and his record has gone before him to judgment.

Dec. 16. — Blessed be God, who has brought me in safety to this city of Liverpool! The day began with a most enjoyable breakfast with the Rev. Mr. Christopher, who made a fine impression on me, as a kind and godly man. After breakfast and a blessed season of family worship, he went with me an hour and a half to see Oxford. Then I took the cars for Stratford-on-Avon, *did* the house of Shakspeare, and at 4.30 P.M. took cars for this place, where I arrived at 9.45 P.M. Oh for grace to be thankful and trustful!

Dec. 25. — Christmas on the ocean! How strange it seems! Kindred and friends are gathered in their homes, and the merry voices of the loving and loved are heard in their mutual greeting, but I am alone on the black, billowy sea. Yet not alone. The Christ-child is here, as well as there; and, in the Divine One, I am linked to many a Christian heart, and sit down at the thanksgiving feast that "unto us a Child is born."

Dec. 28. — The last Sunday of the year, — and on the sea. How like the years of the past is this restless, storm-swept sea! It heaves and swells, it rises into heights, and sinks into depths; it flashes into foam, and lifts its solid columns; it flings its spray aloft, and becomes the chamber of the rainbow; it is a vast expanse of watery peaks with white summits; it is plastic in the mighty hand of some unseen power to take any shape, and do any bidding. Such is human life; changeful, — now rearing the heights of hope, now scooping out the valleys of despondency, passionate, calm, a waste, a beauty, a magnificent something in the hands of a mighty Power that shapes it at will. Yet oh, how good has that Power been in the history of my poor life ! How will I praise Him who has spared the unworthiest, and made my pathway so like the course of this noble ship, that right on through storm and tempest, in the darkness and in the light, amid all commotion and tumult, has obeyed the steady, silent finger that pointed to the desired haven. Oh that henceforth my life may be more than ever resigned to the control of Almighty wisdom and power!

Dec. 31. — What a day of rest and comfort! What a complete fulfilment of desire, and answer to prayer, is here! This last day of the old year is the happiest of them all. Home! that word includes more than I can spread out on paper, or express in words. The relief from care and anxiety, in the forms they have taken for the last few months, the rest from the tossings of the land and sea, the embrace of human sympathy from those that are inexpressibly dear and precious, the wonderful goodness of God in sparing my own life and health and those of my household, the privileges of the year in their passing enjoyment, and in their memory now, the glad hopes, the heavenward desires, the boundless mercies of my Father in countless ways, — all these are about me to-day, to pour peace and happiness into my heart. What shall I render unto God for his unspeakable gifts? Alas! how poorly do I realize these things, compared with their value! How weak and inadequate are my thoughts and feelings, as compared with the sum of my mercies! Lord, I am thine, save me. To thee, *all*.

The following letter was sent by the steamer "Calabria," on the same day on which he sailed on the "Baltic:" —

"LIVERPOOL, Dec. 18, 1873.

"This is my home while in the city. I am off for a far dearer home at 4 P.M., by the White Star steamer 'Baltic.' That earthly home I may never reach, and the beloved embraces of those dearer to me than life I may never realize. But our heavenly Father doeth all things well; and if the joys of an unbroken household be denied us in the wise decrees of his will in our earthly home, the better, heavenly, I trust, is sure. May the last trying hour for each of us. whenever it comes, find us ready to depart and be with Christ, which, however obscure in the dim vision of mortal eyes, and however much the heart may rebel, is far better. And may the peaceful home of the heavenly shore where no storms arise, no ocean rolls, be our blissful portion forever!"

This letter is a good illustration of his never-failing care to foresee, and do all in his power to provide for, every possible emergency or calamity.

CHAPTER VIII.

CALIFORNIA. — METHODIST HYMNAL. — "ADVENTUS SECUN-
DUS." — HYMNAL WITH TUNES. — EXTRACTS FROM SERMONS.

IN the summer of 1875, through the kindness of his old-time friend Dr. L. T. Townsend of Boston University, Mr. Harrington was invited with his wife to join an editorial party for an excursion to the Pacific. The two months thus spent were rich in varied enjoyment. Among these was the continual encounter of old school friends. They were among the first whom we recognized in the party on leaving New York. At Chicago we met the preceptress of Mount Vernon College, Iowa, and found in her one of the graduates at Sanbornton Bridge. On the platform at Omaha, Neb., the county judge claimed acquaintance, and proved himself an old Newbury student. At Oakland, Cal., the projector of the Pacific Railroad introduced himself, and we recognized another pupil from Sanbornton Bridge. And once in San Francisco we had in our hotel a real alumni-meeting of students of Wesleyan.

In the three-weeks' journey across the continent, many expedients were devised to prevent all tediousness of travel. Our cars were transformed into free reading-rooms, social drawing-rooms, literary-club rooms, and Free-Mason lodge-rooms, by turns. After-dinner toasts and jokes were abundant, and fund of conversation of all kinds never wanting.

Botanical, geological, mineralogical, and mining excursions were taken in at all points. Big cities were explored in Christendom, Mormondom, and heathendom; and it was a question whether most alarming tendencies were discovered in Christian cities, in Brigham Young's domains, or in the quarters of the heathen Chinee.

Mr. Harrington entered with enthusiasm into all the opportunities for seeing and learning. He measured the biggest trees, and drank from the waters of the wildest cataracts. He went into the deepest mines, and scaled the highest mountains. He visited the opium-dens, and preached Christ in the Chinese missions. The cream of the whole enjoyment was the visit to Yosemite. Four days were spent in that wonderful temple of Divinity; and in the parlors of a hotel under the overhanging cliffs of mountains eleven thousand feet high, he told the old, old story of the cross, preaching man's redemption by the great God of the universe.

In June, 1876, Professor Harrington received notice that he was one of the fifteen men whom the Board of Bishops, in accordance with a vote of the General Conference, had appointed to revise the Methodist Hymn Book.

He received the appointment as the greatest honor the Church ever had conferred upon him.

Not until after days of prayer, and questioning of his fitness, did he enter tremblingly, but joyfully, upon the important work. As the days went on, and the labors increased, his enthusiasm grew intense, and absorbed every hour that could be spared from his regular college duties. The wealth of sacred song he discovered in the various books the committee were led to examine was an inheritance to his mind and soul, that blessed all his after-life. And when the compilation was completed, it seemed to him that the Church had a new treasure in her hands, that she was very slow to appreciate. Oh, how he loved that Hymnal! It was a store-house of religious joy to him. He wondered and grieved at the modern fashion of merely naming the hymn for the sabbath service; he thought so much effect was produced by the careful and thoughtful reading of those words of doctrine, of worship, of praise, and of holy devotion. It was to him a means of grace that he wished all to enjoy. Many an hour of sleepless night was cheered by the repetition of these songs of the Church.

When the work was nearly completed, it was found a few more hymns were desirable to make just the complement of pages appropriated. Feeling that one subject, which he deemed important, had not been fully represented, he wrote, from a heart full of fervor, the following : —

ADVENTUS SECUNDUS.

When wilt thou come, O Saviour?
   My Lord, when wilt thou come?
My heart is weary waiting,
   And homesick for my home.
Each day mine eyes turn upward,
   And sweep the heavenly plain;
For thine own angels tell me, —
   "He so shall come again."

I tremble at thy thunders,
   That strike my startled sense, —
The amazing conflagration,
   The melting elements.
Yet, bold amid thy terrors,
   My joy my fears shall drown :
I love my Lord's appearing,
   And calmly wait my crown.

Mine eyes o'erflow with weeping,
   At sight of human woe;
My hands hang down with fighting
   The strong and bitter foe.
I'm waiting for the Victor,
   Whose reign is endless day;
I'm waiting the Redeemer,
   Who wipes all tears away.

Perhaps for me thy coming
   Will be through death's dark gate;
I may not see thee yonder
   In clouds and royal state.
E'en as thou wilt, Lord Jesus!
   Thy promise is not slack;
From ages of death's slumber
   Thy voice shall call me back.

Yet come, O blessed Saviour,
   Come quickly, still I pray!
I'm looking for and hasting
   Unto that joyful day;
New heavens and earth in beauty
   Shall spring at thy command;
And I shall see thy glory,
   And with the ransomed stand.

After the Hymnal was completed, and it was decided that the hymns should be set to music, although already weary with the overwork of months, he earnestly coveted the privilege of aiding in this much more laborious task. The committee was smaller; and it was practically left to himself and Dr. F. D. Hemenway of precious memory, to perform the immense amount of drudgery necessary, not merely to select and fit tunes to the hymns, but to fit them to the hymns in their already fixed order in the Hymnal, and under that yoke to arrange metre, style, and melody. The time for this arduous task was limited; for not only were the churches calling for the new Hymn Book, but the committee felt the importance of having the work ready for the supervision of the advisory committee, Professors Tourjée and Holbrook, for whose convenience an especial month had been appointed. This was August, 1877. On the 10th of that month occurred his "silver-wedding" day; and, disappointed at being away on that anticipated anniversary, he sent home these words of cheer: —

"Hail to the silver-wedding day! The voyage of life has brought us to the shore of the silver sea. It has been a pathway of brightness and joy. We touch the waters of the golden sea, and launch to-day on the second quarter-century. How our good Father has blessed us! We have little of silver and gold, but we have what they cannot buy. Let us love and praise the Giver of our joys and mercies more and more. We shall not be likely to see the other shore of the golden sea on earth. We shall celebrate our golden wedding in the city of golden streets, probably. Let us double our diligence to 'make our calling and election sure.' Great love to Karl, the golden bough on our life-tree. May he prove pure gold!"

But no amount of sacrifice or of labor cooled at all his ardor in the accomplishment of that one great desire of his heart, — to have ready for all our churches a book, in which the best sacred songs of the ages should be so united to music, as to promote the highest spiritual life and vigor. He believed music was one of God's best gifts to man, designed to be the agent to lift up his sin-degraded soul into the light and love of divine purity.

And to give music the power designed for it, he believed congregational singing in the churches one of the best methods. That the worship of God by the Church, in the holy songs of Zion, should affect to be accomplished by a paid quartet of perhaps unconsecrated voices, seemed to him both vain and sacrilegious. Singing and music, he said, could and should be as real and effective a part of the worship of God on every Lord's Day, as the sermon and prayers from the pulpit. It was that in which every member of the congregation should feel he had a responsibility and a share. The hope expressed in the last sentence of the Preface to the "Hymnal with Tunes,"— "that the work may stimulate all the people to sing in all the services of the sanctuary, and may contribute somewhat to the spirituality of divine worship through the power of sacred song upon the heart,"— was not merely a written hope: it was an intense longing, and an earnest prayer, the answer to which he never ceased to crave while he lived. For the accomplishment of this desire, he had devoted his whole strength in utter forgetfulness of self, feeling it was a work to which God and the Church had called him; and though the beginning of his downward course in health dated back to that over-strain of his energies, he never regretted that he had given to the work his best powers.

The more recently issued and scholarly "Hymn Studies," by Rev. Charles S. Nutter of the New-Hampshire Conference, he highly appreciated, and greatly enjoyed perusing, wondering if the Church generally were aware of its value.

As the years of his Christian experience increased, his devotion increased for the cross of Christ. Faith in the atonement was the zenith of his creed. He often wondered that that central doctrine was not oftener made the theme of pulpit-teaching. During his last sickness, he always listened with great interest to any one who would report to him a sermon they had heard; and often afterward would say, "Yes, that is all good; but I long to hear more about Jesus and the cross, Jesus and the resurrection. Oh, how I wish I could preach!" he frequently exclaimed. "It seems to me I could make the people see, as I never could before, that it is Jesus' blood that saves from sin."

In one of his sermons he wrote: "In the death of Christ for the sins of mankind, we have the grand culmination of the original decree, the realization of all types and shadows, the literal sacrifice of the Lamb slain from the foundation of the world.

"The decree of God is unmistakable. Whatever be the cavils and objections, the difficulties and mysteries, the word is plain and sure: 'Without shedding of blood is no remission.' Christ's words to his disciples are: 'This is my blood of the New Testament, which is shed for many.' 'In whom we have redemption through his blood,' says Paul to the Ephesians, 'the forgiveness of sins, according to the riches of his grace.' And again, to the Colossians, 'Having made peace through the blood of his cross, it pleased the Father by him to reconcile all things unto himself.' John's testimony is, 'If we walk in the light, as he is in the light, we have fellowship one with another, and the blood of Jesus Christ his Son cleanseth us from all sin.'

"All complaint against this decree is forestalled and forever silenced by the provision of God, made and executed for its fulfilment. He who established the necessity has himself met it. What matters it how hard the conditions of his justice, if they are balanced by his mercy? How could we censure a judge for the severity of his sentence if he at once voluntarily assumed the criminal's place, and suffered in his stead? How could we find fault with a sovereign for making any law whose penalty he suffers himself that his offending subjects may not suffer? If man had been remedilessly left to bear the penalty of his own sins with his own blood, wonder at such a merciless severity might have begotten desperation and sullen defiance. If heartless and implacable Fate had driven its iron chariot-wheels over bleeding humanity, humanity might well have cursed the gory monster with its dying breath. If godless law, as some, in these days of advanced thought, will have it, has developed the human race for self-butchery during its earthly career, and painful extinction at last, the race might be pardoned for vainly raging at such a shedding of blood *without* remission. The mystery and terror that cover mere law and blind fate are a thousand-fold greater than attach to the sovereignty of an all-wise God.

"Let the earth rejoice in the reign of a just God. Let the earth doubly rejoice in the reign of a God of mercy. If blood must atone, the blood of atonement is at hand.

"By such a provision, moreover, the wisdom and righteousness of God are vindicated. The decree that ordains the remission of sin by the shedding of blood, was made in full view of the Divine method and purpose to fulfil it. It could not have been any thing short of necessity, governed by infinite wisdom and righteousness, that issued a decree which must cost the blood of the Son of

God. It was no slight demand that could coolly ordain the suffering of the Creator in the creature's stead. In the clear light of the incarnation, with all it involved of humility and shame, beholding the bloody sweat of Gethsemane and the wounds of Calvary, realizing the agony of the hiding of the Father's face, and the darkness of the sepulchre, He who was to endure it all pronounced the word, 'without the shedding of blood is no remission.' If a milder penalty for sin could have been devised, if less than death were possible for crime that would rob God of his throne, would he have ordained it? Would he have made it mean more than needful to be 'despised and rejected of men,' to be 'a man of sorrows and acquainted with grief'? Was it a needless work, that he was 'wounded for our transgressions, and bruised for our iniquities'? Did he submit to torture without a cause?

"Without his sacrifice, the world might have paused and questioned. Isaac's wondering query on Mount Moriah, 'Where is the lamb for the burnt offering?' would have been the unanswered cry of the ages, as generation after generation paid its own penalty of blood. Abraham's unwavering reply, 'God will provide himself a lamb,' was faith's all-satisfying answer, prophetic then, but now forevermore accomplished. The Old-Testament text, 'Thou shalt surely die,' finds its ample explanation in the Revelator's comment, 'the Lamb slain from the foundation of the world.'

"The mystery of sin and death is solved by the greater mystery of redemption. As two hard, dark substances sometimes flash into flame when brought into contact, so, from spiritual affinities, two eternal mysteries, brought into contact with each other, evolve the glorious light that floods the world with mercy, salvation, and love."

It was not in his sermons alone that the wonderful plan of redemption was mentioned. It was an ever-present thought with him, interwoven in his every-day life. In one of his familiar letters to a sister, he says, "How in the world I succeed in keeping up my end of the yoke in the matter of letter-writing to your family, is a marvel to me. Why, there are six of you against one! Wonder how many I owe now? Well, never mind: if I get hopelessly in debt, I expect you will forgive the debt. That is the only way I can get square in many of my failures in this world. And I am more and more thankful that our good Father can do the same for all the follies of life. I do not understand the great mystery of pardon through a Saviour; but it is that or nothing for my poor soul, and there I hang my hope. That hope ought to grow brighter and sweeter every day, for the days are flying. But so stupendous a mercy, and so infinite a work wrought for only dust and ashes, defiled at that, sometimes staggers me. I mean, however, that death shall find me under the light of the cross, beholding the Lamb of God that taketh away the sin of the world."

In an address delivered on the death of President Garfield, he says, "The life of our redeeming Lord was the sum of all perfection, and his example worthy the imitation of the race. But his sufferings and death were their salvation. It is the *cross* of Christ in which all his disciples glory. It was ordained that even the Son of man should be made perfect through suffering. Men admire and honor his stainless character, his self-denying poverty, his ever-active benevolence, and the divine wisdom of his words; but it is at the foot of the cross that they sit in wondering love, and reverent, tearful worship. And in the worship of heaven, according to the record of Revelation, the song is, 'Worthy is the Lamb that was *slain*, to receive power and riches and wisdom and strength and honor and glory and blessing.'"

In all his later sermons, it was his constant, earnest, longing effort to show clearly the simple faith of Jesus; to teach what is meant by evangelical conversion; and to convince all, if possible, that this old gospel truth is still the truth of God. From a sermon on 1 Cor. ii. 14, is taken the following extract: —

"When through the study of the divine history, which is the simple revelation of God's love to man in the gift of his Son for the sin of the world, and which, stripped of all abstraction and imagination, is the essence of the gospel, — when, through the study of this, God's Spirit begets a gospel-faith in the heart, then the one knowledge which science can never give by gradual processes enters the soul. It is the knowledge of Christ as a personal Redeemer: as real and tangible as any other truth. That there is such a knowledge, a distinct and separate fact, as real and cognizable as any other fact, is the foundation rock on which the whole fabric of salvation is built. It is the first item of the things of the Spirit of God, which the faith-faculty reveals, and is the key to all the rest. He who denies that conversion is a real change, having definite characteristics and appreciable evidences — that regeneration is not a shadowy dream, nor a figment of the imagination, but a matter of personal consciousness and knowledge, denies the accumulated testimony of unnumbered multitudes all along the line of Christian history, and the express declaration of the Divine Word, which is the authority for the whole plan of salvation. With this doctrine Christianity stands or falls. When this is surrendered, the citadel is surrendered. It is the sole distinction between Christianity and heathenism. It is the belief of the soundest divines, that the whole Christian Church in the first centuries enjoyed it, and that all the reformed churches in Europe once believed it. Luther, Calvin, Melanchthon, Arminius, Wesley, insisted upon it. Says Sherlock, 'I desire those who think they have no need to trouble their heads about conversion by faith in Jesus Christ, to consider the character of Cornelius. He was devout, and feared God with all his house; gave much alms to the people, prayed to God always: and yet there needed to be a vision to Cornelius, another to Peter, preaching by Peter, the descent of the Holy Ghost, and baptism, to make Cornelius a Christian.' Inspiration says, 'Hereby we *know* that he abideth in us, by the Spirit which he hath given us.' When, by receiving Christ, power is given to become the sons of God, when peace is given for turmoil and unrest, when a heart of flesh replaces a stony heart, when, in a new creation, old things pass away, and all things become new, — certainly, changes are wrought as definite and real as the transition from sickness to health, or from dungeon darkness to the broadest sunlight. If there is any direct or explicit language in the Scriptures, it is that which describes this change." Farther on, he says, "Conversion is a simple, round fact, uncombined, uncompounded, unamalgamated, of which men have knowledge by faith."

From the last sermon he wrote, on Phil. iii. 9, are taken the following extracts : —

"What is the faith that makes men righteous?

"Negatively, it is the faith that cuts loose from every object save Jesus Christ. It has no collateral reliance. It does not prop itself up by braces that reach away to various foundations. It does not fortify itself by Quaker guns, nor kindle false fires of strategy. It has no temporary defences, where it may hide and skirmish, away from its stronghold and impregnable last resort. It does not scout curiously or wantonly into the regions of imagination or reason, to toy and dally with uncertainties and possibilities, and the dangerous snares of its enemies. It borrows no support from material nature, or the nature of man, or the nature of God. It does not strengthen itself by appealing, as grounds for consideration, to the eternal harmonies, to hereditary fatalistic bias, to circumstantial hinderances, to the mysteries of human history and human destiny, or to the attributes of the Divine character. It does not allege a moral life, a hard lot, an unbelieving tendency, an amiable or benevolent disposition, as virtual objects of faith, in that they partially or entirely excuse the imperfection or absence of faith in the only proper object of it. It does not substitute the life of Christ, his spotless character, or his marvellous teachings, for the cross of Christ, the essential, central object of faith.

"It is a faith that utterly renounces all dependence upon ourselves. It recognizes without qualification our lost, undone, helpless condition. For, otherwise, we should claim to be partners with God in the redemption of the soul. Christ would not be the *Saviour* of men, but only an assistant in their moral improvement. He could not be the giver of life, unless men were dead. Salvation is a misnomer for the gospel scheme, unless sinners are hopeless.

"It is a faith that recognizes the depravity of our nature, our actual guilt, and the justice of God in his judgment of sin. It confesses squarely and honestly our ill-desert, and the righteousness of God in the execution of the penalties he has denounced against the sinner. To do less than this, would be to charge God with overestimating our guilt, and making a superfluous or unnecessary provision against an unreal danger, and demanding more than our need warrants.

"The faith that makes men righteous is the faith that fastens simply and trustingly on the Lord Jesus Christ as the only, all-sufficient, atoning Saviour. To that faith it is Jesus that blots our transgressions, makes our record clear. It is Jesus that *gives* spiritual life. It is he that *continues* it. This faith merges the believer's life in the life of Christ. It dares not, it wishes not, a moment's separation. It knows no historic past; it deals only in present tenses. It echoes Paul's prayer, 'Let me *be found in him*.' It sees that to be found there is to be a partaker of the divine nature. As a polluted drop of water loses its filth in the ocean, so it sees the soul's unrighteousness disappear in the infinite righteousness of Christ; and, as the drop is kept pure in the bosom of the sea, so is the soul kept pure in the embrace of infinite purity. It is in Jesus that the soul finds holy living, constant victory over self and sin, the world, the flesh, and the Devil. . . .

"The wondering question, 'How can these things be?' begins with Nicodemus, and ends with Thomas, in the gospel history. Neither the master in Israel with all his learning, nor the disciple of Jesus under the living voice of the great Teacher, has explained it to the understanding. Apostolic wisdom has only set forth the facts and results of a spiritual experience, and left its philosophy unrevealed.

"It is the riddle of the ages. Millions have fallen upon this stone, and been broken; on millions it has fallen, and ground them to powder. No answer has ever been heard but the answer of the believing heart. It has contained no explanation of processes. It has only been a living witness of the fact. Somehow, in all generations, when the finger of faith has touched the Saviour's garment, and the voice of faith has said, 'My Lord and my God,' the marvellous change has been wrought, and the sinner, in the filthy rags of his own righteousness, has become clothed in the royal robes of Christ's righteousness. He may not be wise enough to explain the philosophy or the method; but he is a witness to the great work, and his whole soul adopts Jude's inspired language, 'Now unto Him that is able to present me faultless before the presence of his glory with exceeding joy, to the only wise God our Saviour, be glory and majesty, dominion and power, both now and ever.'

"It would seem strange, to one utterly unacquainted with the conditions behind it, that the poorest man on earth, by presenting a bit of paper at the counter of a banking-house, indorsed by the single name of one of our countrymen, might instantly become possessed of millions, not by any thing that he had done, or could do, but solely by the virtue of that name. But it only dimly shadows forth the power of that Name by which the poorest sinner of us all may be made, in a moment, richer than all earth's riches. It is gloriously true, and we can have some conception of it, that the humblest citizen can wrap himself in the stars and stripes, and traverse the globe, stand in the presence of kings and emperors, face all the power of arms and laws, and everywhere command respect, and everywhere defy harm or injustice. It is not in him, but the flag of his country robes him in the strength of a mighty nation. But it faintly illustrates how the humblest saint, clothed in the robe of Christ's righteousness, may stand fearless before principalities and powers, and the rulers of the darkness of this world, and even the arch-enemy of souls, and defy his power to harm or do him wrong. He wears the royal garment of Him who can be just, and the justifier of him who believeth in Jesus.

"I cannot tell the process. I cannot explain the power by which the black coal is transformed into the gleaming diamond: how much less can I tell how, by the mystery of the new birth, the lost, dead soul lives by the merit of Jesus! I cannot tell how the living tree gets its flower and fruit from the dead substance in which it is rooted, and on which it feeds: how much less can I tell how the wounds, the blood, the death of Christ, give life to the soul dead in trespasses and sins, and clothe it with the fruitage of holiness! Or how can I tell the end of this divine work, when the Giver of spiritual life shall crown it with life eternal; when dust and ashes — this body — shall spring from its sepulchre, and appear in the glorified body of the resurrection? But it shall be done, according to the working of the power whereby he is able to subdue all things unto himself. Enough for me that this is God's way, and the work is worthy of God. The righteousness may be mine by the faith of Jesus Christ. 'Not by works of righteousness that we have done, but according to his mercy, he saved us by the washing of regeneration and the renewing of the Holy Ghost.' Faithful is he that hath promised, who also will do it."

CHAPTER IX.

KARL.—BIRTHDAY POEM.—LETTERS.—DIARIES.—CLASS-MEETINGS. — SICKNESS. — VACATION. — LETTERS. — NEW-HAMPSHIRE CONFERENCE.

IN the year 1882 occurred his only boy's graduation from college. He had watched the four years' course with the intensity of interest that only a Christian parent can know. He understood so well the snares, the pitfalls, the lions in the way. His constant prayer was that his boy might pass through this test period with body unimpaired, with mind well stored and disciplined, and with soul unscathed. He had consecrated him to God at his birth. April 4, 1869, his diary reads, "To-day our dear boy wishes and intends to go forward in the sacrament of baptism. He is a child, and has the light-heartedness and impulsiveness of a child; but I think he has also a childlike faith in Jesus as his Saviour. Doubtless he has not the deep and clear comprehension of the meaning of the rite, that adult years will bring; but that is no reason why he should wait for the years to come before he devotes his young heart to Jesus. Oh that God may receive him and bless him!" A year later, on the day of his joining the Methodist Episcopal Church, in full membership, a note of the fact is closed with, "Oh that in the Church militant he may war a good warfare, and win a glorious crown!" June 13, of 1882, completed Karl's twenty-first year; and his father's birthday gift was accompanied with an expression of his thoughts at that time: —

> "O childhood, boyhood, youth, thy years, —
>   Prelude and pledge of manhood's prime, —
> With all their joys and hopes and fears,
>   Are garnered with the sheaves of Time.
> With hurrying footsteps, one by one,
>   Ye trooped behind the restless Now,
> That double veil of night and sun,
>   Which flings its gloom o'er the cold brow
> Of lifeless years; but flames its beams
>   Of buoyant hope on Time's last-born,
> As if *that* would not swell the stream
>   Gone by, or night not follow morn.
> And darker through the fourscore sum
>   On life's first stage the pall shall rest,
> As echoes faint and fainter come,
>   Repeated from each mountain breast.
> Yet, O young years, a score and one,
>   An immortality is yours!
> Essential life, now just begun,
>   Unending while the soul endures.
> Only the gross and mortal clay
>   Is sepulchred behind the veil;
> The soul of Time must ever stay
>   To set its seal, and tell its tale.
> As diamonds gleaned from worthless sand,
>   Or golden grains in torrent-bed,
> So may these years, with liberal hand,
>   Leave only blessings on thy head.
> And if God give thee length of days,
>   And fill them with a gracious store,
> Be all thy years his psalm of praise
>   Thy benediction evermore."

June 29 the diary says, " It is the commencement day of life with us, in that Karl is to graduate. How indescribable are the emotions that run along the nerve-track, and thrill the hearts of fathers and mothers to-day!"

June 30. — The show is over. With thanksgiving to God, be it recorded that mercy and goodness have been abundantly shown to us and ours in all the anxieties and labors of these days. The Lord is good.

Aug. 4, he wrote to his sister : —

"Lizzie invites me to increase the bulk of her letter to the extent of half a sheet. Probably she has told you all the news about the condition of the household, both as to the pleasure of the past and the contrast of the present. The pleasure of the past has been heightened not a little by the presence of Mary. And now that she and Karl have disappeared, the desolation is quite considerable. So we are solacing ourselves as well as we can by keeping busy, and writing letters to our friends for an episode in our regular work. Sometimes I wish I had more friends, so that I might enjoy the pleasure of more visits; and sometimes I wish that I had none, so that I might be spared the pain of parting from them. But the mixture of pain and pleasure, good and evil, in all things earthly, is God's law, ordained, no doubt, in wisdom for the welfare of his creatures. The 'what for' is none of our business, if the fact be so. The sooner we can come to the point of accepting the situation, of eating from this table of the Divine spreading, 'asking no questions for 'conscience' sake,' or any other sake, the better it will be for our peace. It is always 'hard to kick against the pricks.' The lesson is plain; but, oh, what slow learners we are!

"My time, these days, is variously divided between

house, dooryard, and college, with suitable episodes downtown and to the religious services; all of which divisions are, doubtless, of no importance to you. Sometimes life seems bright, and sometimes dark, which is a common experience, and no news. Yet all these little insignificances have their meaning and bearing on others' lives, else I should not be writing this little nothing to you. How strange that each other's littles make up so large a part of each other's whole! Every thing is strange in this world. Nothing is strange in this world. Isn't this a moralizing, paradoxical letter?"

Aug. 18, he wrote the following to a niece: —

"We are Block-Islanders, you see. No connection with the block-*head* family. It is only a temporary expedient to escape the heat of home for a few days, and try what effect the change of air may have on our heads and nerves. If it makes our heads wiser, and our nerves stronger, it will pay. . . . We had a fine sail hither, and it is as cool and beautiful this afternoon as one could wish.

> I've just been down by the sounding sea,
>   And watched the waves come in;
> And they murmured their sea-song tenderly,
>   As if they'd a soul within;
> And the rocks on the shore stood white and bare
>   Save their tresses of seaweed green,
> And the ripples toyed with their tresses fair
>   As the tide rose and sunk again;
> And the heaving waves caught my thoughts away
>   From the pebbly sea-washed strand,
> And wafted them over the watery spray
>   To the friends of a far-off land.

"That is all the rhyming I can afford to do to-night But I wish you could enjoy the sea view from our Spring House veranda, as it stretches away, and spreads to the right and left, and loses our gaze at last in the far east, where the clear sun-line cuts the sky. It is beautiful, and the air is cool; and there is blue above, and blue beneath. The young moon is in the west, and the stars crop out one by one, — the thoughtful, faith-inspiring stars of God. Nature is full of good suggestions, but the buzz of conversation around us is little in harmony with it. I wonder if Nature and human society are often in harmony. Things seem sadly out of joint sometimes, but I guess it is due to the perversity of poor human nature chiefly. . . .

"I do hope the purpose you formed that Sunday evening will prove a point of departure for a decided upgrade, and a richer experience. Strike out into deeper water, and trust the Lord to help you swim, and perhaps even to walk on the water, by his mighty help. Forget self, and go out after somebody who shall be a star in the crown of your rejoicing."

On the morning of April 13, of this year, he had been seized with a sudden and very severe chill, that was followed by a fever, which kept him from his work for three weeks. And though he seemed to recover fully from it, and during the year to be as vigorous as usual, yet he said himself afterward, "I think my health was breaking in the summer of 1882. I am sure I was not myself then, either physically or mentally. In no other way can I account for certain experiences at that time."

Jan. 1, 1883, his diary says: "The transition to the new year makes no jostle of earthly conditions. The swing of the planet is peaceful and steady. Hope is still the star in the east. Purpose still clings to the word of God, and to the Saviour of men."

Jan. 28. — My day in college chapel. I go to the duty with some different feelings from those I had at one time. I would use the opportunity to deliver God's message to man in a way that shall please him. The ranks of Satan's army are full, and their vast numbers make their very inertia immense in power. There is no hope save in God, who can make "one to chase a thousand, and two put ten thousand to flight."

Feb. 10. — We had a good meeting last night. Its feature was the evident presence of the Holy Spirit in unusual power. Thank God! Oh that he would stir this wicked place to its foundations! Lord, awaken sinners.

This refers to one of the meetings of his church-class, held on Friday night. That class was his Bethel. He went to it weekly with the anticipation of a child to his home; and he left it with the refreshing of soul that came from having met his Lord. He often wondered how any one who knew what communion of saints meant, or who had any sense of being lifted up by the power of united faith into the presence of Jesus, could deny himself the privilege of attending a weekly religious class-meeting. "I cannot understand it," he would say. "I don't believe they are aware of the wonderful power of Christian communion." How often he urged upon young Christians the importance of improving this means of grace in our church! And to students, who sometimes pleaded want of time, he frequently quoted the example of an associate professor, who had evidently lost no power as a scholar, though during the four years of his college course he was scarcely once missed from this weekly meeting.

During the spring vacation, a cold and fever kept him in bed for five days. On the day of opening the term, he wrote: "My strength is not up to the normal, but I guess I am strong enough to begin. Give me, O Lord, a thankful heart for all I have, and grace to do all thy will in future. Especially keep me from besetting sin."

June 1. — The beauty of the day is a promise for the month. It will be one of trial and hard work. It will need patience and self-control. I pray for help. With all the conviction that to die is to live, it is hard work to do it.

But the "trial and hard work" were of a different nature from what he expected. That night he came home severely chilled, and before morning was in a burning fever, that kept him in bed during the whole month, and in extreme suffering. Every effort to conquer the disease seemed unavailing. Day by day suffering increased and strength decreased, and night after night hope grew less; until, one midnight hour, he thought his work was done, and he must make ready to go. Having expressed his wishes as far as possible, with trembling voice he sang, —

> "Abide with me! fast falls the eventide,
> The darkness deepens: Lord, with me abide.
> When other helpers fail, and comforts flee,
> Help of the helpless! oh, abide with me."

The Helper came, and disease yielded slowly to medical treatment. During the month of July he began to move about his room, and finally gained strength to join the family circle. One morning, after a bath, he suddenly discovered that there was no apparent action in his right lung. His physician was called to examine it, who at once acknowledged the fact, and gave little hope that the organ would ever regain its use; though, he said, many years of life and labor might continue without it. This was a terrible trial. "To make up one's mind," he said, "that life henceforth is to be the life of an invalid, a life of endurance, of crippled powers, unfit to battle in the conflicts of strong men, is exceedingly humiliating, and requires great store of grace."

July 27 he wrote the following, in a letter to a niece: "I find, in looking over my unanswered letters, that your last one is among the number. It was dated two days before I was taken sick. . . .

"Since then I have been nearer than ever before, so far as I know, to the great divide that separates the continents of life and death. One looks both ways in such a case, and while the eye lingers on the familiar scenes and faces of the sense-world, it also throws many glances at the world unseen. The nearer view intensifies the interest in the unexplored unknown, and begets heart-searching in the depths where the soul's secrets and its real condition have never been so fully realized before. So I hope the discipline of sickness will make me a better man, and more fit for heaven by and by."

The first week in August, with his family, he took the little voyage from New York to Portland. He loved the sea, and all the effect of the voyage acted like a charm upon his strength. Encouraged by this, we went to Old Orchard, and spent two weeks looking for a continuance of improvement. He hoped much from sea-bathing, in which he had formerly revelled. Once, for a moment, he tried its effect here, but only to be convinced he could not endure it. The heat was oppressive, and he lost the good gained on the voyage.

Thence we went to the summit of Mount Pleasant, in Bridgeton, Me., and spent about ten days. These were days of great encouragement. The air was health and strength. The place was quiet and delightful. The guests were intelligent and social. We strolled over the mountain wilds, sat on the rocks and read in the sunlight, and never tired of gazing at the grand array of White Mountains that stretched all along the horizon, on the one hand, or the varied summer scenery that lay, a bright parorama, on the other. Our time there was all too short; but the end of summer vacation drew near, and no arguments could induce him to be away from his classes at the beginning of the college year. He returned to his post of duty, and persistently, throughout the year, prosecuted his usual work, though contending constantly with physical weakness, and more or less pain. Changes in the weather were keenly felt; and other annoyances, that formerly he met with cheerful courage, were heavy burdens. This physical suffering affected his spiritual life, so that the year was one of conflict, without the usual victories.

Jan. 28, 1884, he wrote: —

"'Fight on, my soul, till death,
Nor lay thine armor down.'

"Since that is God's will, it is best not to murmur, I suppose, but try to keep step to the battle-march."

Jan. 30. — "'These all died in faith.' The best men of whom we have any record have gone down with no other light. Let us not, then, complain, but accept the doctrine as cheerfully as possible."

The following letter to his sister was written on Feb. 6 : —

"It rains outside, and so I am cheated out of my prayer-meeting. I'll have a quiet chat with you, then, instead, and pay my debt. . . .

"I am glad the world has some good people in it. Sometimes I think they are very few, — only just enough to save it from another rain of fire and brimstone. This is in my pessimistic moments, when the rascality of rum-sellers, the greed of politicians, or the lying tricks of all sorts of selfish people, absorb my thoughts. At other times, I am ready to admit that there are a great many people who are a great deal better than they seem to be, and perhaps thousands on thousands who are the Lord's freemen, though they seem to be Satan's slaves. This is when my charity is in full bloom, and my estimate of myself is far below zero. Which is the better view to take, the nearest correct in point of fact, and the most beneficial to us? Don't you ever catch yourself saying to yourself, 'Well, if I can be saved, then nobody need despair;' 'If so poor a Christian as I can be counted one of God's children, then anybody can'? Maybe you don't; but I have occasional musings of that sort, and don't feel like judging the meanest creature on earth. Do you ever wonder how, in even the infinite power and mercy of God, he can make our vile human nature fit for a holy heaven and the holy fellowship of Christ and his saints? It seems to me one of the greatest mysteries of the plan of salvation. But then, of what use to dwell on the mysteries of our faith? The only way to get even a crumb of comfort out of the plan of salvation is to make faith the single, central, sole personal fact with ourselves. Naked faith is the only reliance. We must persuade ourselves that it has ample foundation, and exercise it. Let every thing else go. Shut eyes and ears and all the senses to all the clamors of world, flesh, and Devil, and be everlastingly content to be called fools for Christ's sake. I don't see that any harm can come of it. We shall be as well off as those other fools who call us so. They tread round in their little half-bushel of reason and doubt and speculation, and never *know* any thing after all. And the grave will soon end all, and test all. 'Let me die the death of the righteous, and let my last end be like his.'"

The diary of March 14 has: "What can be more desirable for a human being, fully aware of the conditions of that being, than to have a clear, unwavering faith in the great doctrines of God, heaven, and immortality? 'Lord, increase my faith.' The unbelief of our hearts is amazing. The key to our indifference, our worldliness, and our sinfulness, in many ways, is a practical unbelief in what we profess to believe. We need to cultivate our faith greatly."

March 5 he wrote again: —

"Probably the chief interest you will take in this letter will be the consciousness that somebody, away off in the

State of Connecticut, has remembered a debt, and proceeds to pay it. As to the matter of it, my brain is in that comatose state when ideas are scarce or dormant. But then, I console myself with the generous reflection that ideas are scarce with most people at times; and in a good many cases, — though I should not dare to say it of Plymouth people, — ideas are troublesome, and require too much hard work to manage them. It is especially hard to get up an original idea in this age of the world. Pretty much all we have have filtered down through the ages, and are either worn so smooth as to have no distinguishable stamp on them, or discolored by various combinations, or are now and then purified and made more usable. They go jingling along through the brains of people, and sometimes get a new impetus, and strike us more forcibly for having been re-minted and made bright. It is probably fortunate that each generation thinks itself wiser than the last, though it may be self-flattery. It is not well to let hope die out of the generations, nor of the individuals who compose them. But who can look at the contradictions and differences in human opinion, at the theories advanced and abandoned, at the guess-work of so-called philosophers, and the quarrels of scientists, and be greatly encouraged at the progress of absolute knowledge or the certainties of human attainment? When we look at the condition of human nature, we find that the story of sin and depravity is 'the old, old story' as truly as is the story of 'Jesus and his love.' Verily, Solomon was right in saying, 'There is nothing new under the sun.' Well, then, what have we to do but make the best of the old? Nothing, of course. But it isn't always easy to know how to do it, that is the bother. We are continually making mistakes, even when we mean to do the best, to say nothing of those errors that spring from perversity or selfishness. What in the world should we do if we had no faith in the compassion of Him who remembers that we are dust? If we can only, amid all the perplexities and discouragements about us, believe that our Father is guiding us through all the mazes of our mystery, and pardoning and pitying us in our ignorance and helplessness, it is a consolation full of peace and rest. But, alas! the vast majority of us do not really believe it. We think we do, but we do not. Such a faith *must* bring a perfect willingness to let the world wag as it will, and a perfect superiority to all the ups and downs, hithers and thithers, of this storm-tossed life. Don't you think so? Look the ground over, and see if faith is not the immense lack of our earthly life."

April 4, he wrote in his diary: "In New York, at the St. Denis. The usual feeling of loneliness in a great city is upon me. Nobody knows, nobody cares for the stranger. The world is nothing without love."

April 5. — Home again. It is always a joy to be welcomed after an absence, and *home* is a sweeter word than ever, the nearer we get to the eternal home on high. Lord, help me to live for that!

April 6. — The burden of the morning communion-service falls on me this conference Sunday. Thank God for strength enough to bear it! And, oh that wisdom and grace may be given from God to make the service a blessing to the people.

April 7. — He hears and answers prayer. Thanks be to God for so much faith as I have. Oh that it were vastly greater! We start to-day for Conference. It is a little perilous, but I hope for the defence and blessing of God upon all.

This refers to the New-Hampshire Conference, which opened its session at Manchester on April 9. He seemed fully confident that it would be his last opportunity to meet his own Conference, and he was very anxious to do so "*once more.*" All through the different exercises of the week, there was recurring the same thought, — "It will be the last time." He enjoyed it as a kind of continual leave-taking, growing every day more weary. April 15, he wrote: "At home. It seems very good to be in the old haunts and paths. A little while, and the roaming will cease forever. There will be a going-out without return. Let me keep that day suitably in mind."

June 17. — The first sign of blood from throat, lungs, or somewhere about my breathing apparatus, appeared this morning. I am not sure but it is the beginning of the end. There is no better way than to look every state and every event calmly in the face. There are inevitable things that cannot be turned aside, and some things that can be averted by wisdom.

CHAPTER X.

CENTENNIAL OF MIDDLETOWN. — POEM. — VACATION. — DIARY. — LETTER. — PARTIAL COLLEGE WORK. — "TO NELLIE ON HER WEDDING-DAY." — BATTLE WITH DISEASE. — "WHAT IS YOUR LIFE?" — OLD CHURCH.

ON July 14, 1884, the city of Middletown celebrated its first centennial. No child in all the streets, probably, anticipated the event more than did the invalid professor.

Always fond of good music of any kind, he was especially charmed with martial music; and combined with this, the perfect order, steady tread, and uniform dress of militia had a strange fascination that often quite overcame him. Seated in an easy-chair so far down the lawn in front of his door, as that he might be undisturbed by the merry chatter of the group collected on the veranda, he remained motionless as company after company of the long pageant trooped by, until, fearing he might become exhausted, I ventured to steal beside him. The tears were rolling down his cheeks; and when I said, "Are you having a good time?" with childish satisfaction he replied, "Oh, yes; don't interrupt me," and continued in that rapt state during the whole hour in which the procession was passing. Afterward he said, "Maybe you think it weak; but I cannot explain the strange power military music and display has over me." He longed to contribute something to the success of the interesting day; and after composing a hymn, which was sung on the occasion, he wrote the following little poem, which he said was of no use except to gratify his own interest : —

On this green slope of beauty rare,
    Laved by the river's happy flow,
Sprung to its birth a city fair,
    This day a hundred years ago.

Not massive wall, nor moat, nor tower,
    Were its foundation and defence;
But men of heart, and men of power,
    Girded with God's omnipotence.

For civic weal in Christian lands,
    And arts of peace with laws benign,
No bulwarks need, or mail-clad bands,
    But virtue's arm and truth divine.

A hundred years through sire and son,
    Of honest toil with hand and brain,
Of wealth increased and honors won,
    Of life and death, of woe and pain.

A hundred years of honored share
    Among her peers in war and peace;
In war her country's flag to bear,
    In council wise when wars should cease.

Let but her classic shades abide,
    Let busy arts find here a home,
Religion be her people's guide,
    In generations yet to come;

Then not a hundred years alone
    Shall celebrate her honored name;
Not ancient Troy, nor haughty Rome,
    Shall equal her enduring fame.

Two days later, he started with his family on a long vacation trip which he had planned, to include visits to several of his kindred; saying, "If I can endure it, it will be a great satisfaction to me, as well as to them, to look in on their homes once more." Setting his will at defiance to pain and fatigue, he entered into all the sources of enjoyment with cheerfulness, determined to make this — our last pleasure-trip — the happiest of them all. He revelled in the novelties of the new home of his only brother in Bradford, Penn., studying with interest the wonders of that strange oil-region, watching the perilous process of "shooting" an oil-well, examining with particular minuteness the noted Kinzua bridge, three hundred and one feet in height, — said to be the highest in the world, — joined with delight in the family concerts, and the rehearsals of old-time experiences. On July 28, for the first time in many months, and the last time in his life, he preached a sermon, from Luke xviii. 8. Thence we went to the homes of his step-mother and his two sisters in Syracuse, N.Y., where all that loving hearts could devise rendered the days happy. A visit to the saltworks, a picnic on the lake-shore, rides about the delightful city, all added to the pleasure of kindred communion. The journey continued then by way of Thousand Island Park, St. Lawrence and its wonderful rapids, and Montreal, to St. Johnsbury, Vt., "the home of his boyhood." Here resting for a day, he called on all who remembered the "Calvin" of earlier years. The warm greetings and pleasant rehearsal of memories, the visit to the house where he was born, the familiar sound of the rushing milldam, a stroll over the old farm, and especially a ramble in First Woods, where, seated by the cool spring, he recalled the scenes of his childhood and youth, — all these rendered the time sacredly delightful. Then a few pleasant days in the home of a sister-in-law in New Hampshire, and a few more of sympathy with a sadly bereaved brother-in-law, and we reached our home, Aug. 25, finding that the journey had not apparently depleted his strength.

Sept. 11, the diary says: "Term begins. By the grace and mercy of God, I am able to begin my college work. May the same grace and mercy continue and help me to do all I do 'heartily, as unto the Lord, and not as unto men.' Oh for Divine help *all* the time!"

Sept. 15. — Fighting the cold weather with poor condition of body, and no provision for the severe beginnings of cold weather at college. It is a little hard to stand the strain. I'll do my best, with God's help.

Sept. 16. — But here I am at home sick, disabled, and my work goes by the board. Well, I must make the best of it, and still trust in the Lord, and wait.

Sept. 24, in a letter to his brother, he says, —

"I am not feeling very mighty to-day, so you may not get a very eloquent letter. I got a mysterious pull-back just before that hot spell came on, and all through that I was pretty flat. But, three or four days before the term began, I began to pick up, and felt pretty well. I commenced my work in college with a good deal of courage and hope. But alas! that cold snap! It took me down worse than the 'killing frost' in Dick Farnham's declamation. So, since last Monday, I've been an unwilling prisoner at home. I hardly know what ails me. The last cold, I think, is about conquered; but the dregs of a fever seem to be hanging about me, which I would a good deal rather see hanging in some other place. The thing doesn't budge, and I'm in for an enforced absence from my classes, whereat the scowl of impatience and the smile of submission are, I fear, ludicrously mingled. Such is the situation with this child."

When about to resume his classes, his associate professors most kindly arranged to relieve him from one class during the term, leaving him only two, that recited on alternate days. This amount of work, then, he assumed on Oct. 9, and prosecuted it during the remainder of the college year.

During the whole month of December, there was an apparent improvement in his health, which so encouraged him, that he wrote on Dec. 25 : —

"Merry Christmas. In good health as a household, in peace and plenty, in love and fellowship with all, in good hope of everlasting life through Christ, whom we adore to-day, I find abundant reason for sacred gratitude and innocent mirth."

Early in January, however, the persistent hand of disease grasped tighter, and every day was one of weariness and struggle. On Jan. 27, in a letter to his sister, after speaking of others in the household, he says, —

"As for me, the third and most important member of this large and noted household, I have eaten and drunken, lounged and slept, done considerable coughing, read Latin, heard one recitation at college, written two letters, read the papers, and received calls. Probably this describes to you the state of my health as well as if I should go into a technical diagnosis, with the proper thumpings of breast, back, and bowels, and report to you item by item. I am battling for life and health, just as all the rest of the world are, and grim Death at last gets the seeming victory.

> "By death I shall escape from death,
> And life eternal gain."

Feb. 3, his journal has this entry: —

"Nellie Prentice Merrill died yesterday morning, and is to be buried to-day. The long struggle is over, and she is at home. 'I shall see you when I get home,' were her last words to me. Does she see?"

Nellie was one of his favorites. The great sorrow that came into her child-life, the beauty of soul it developed, her early-wasting health, her resolute braving of disease, her happy marriage only about a month before she went home, — all these he had watched with loving interest. On the morning of her marriage he sent her the following little poem: —

TO NELLIE, ON HER WEDDING-DAY.

> Yes, it's only a holy linking
> Of hearts long since one in love,
> Just a seal divine, I'm thinking,
> In the register up above.
>
> But it pledges an arm strong and tender,
> A resting-place on a stout heart,
> In sickness or health a defender;
> A soul-joy naught else can impart.

So the Christmas-tide blessing be on you,
  And the new year bring with it new life;
And the perils that threaten the maiden
  Flee away, now the maid is a wife.

And when the good Father shall sever
  The bond that he hallows to day,
His bridal shall bless you forever
  With pleasures that pass not away.

His diary, at this time, has frequent reference to his own health: —

March 14. — The ailments of the body become in time like the fetters of the slave, — almost a part of ourselves. We shall never know complete freedom until the clay-clods are shaken off.

March 21. — The desire to live, and the dread of death are so strong in human nature, that the most terrible pains and distress are endured rather than death. A thousand deaths are suffered rather than one. If God be for us, who can be against us? If we try our best to secure his favor and mercy, why not be at peace? To be on the anxious stretch is wearing and discouraging. Keep a good conscience, and trust him for all.

April 10. — Went to prayers yesterday morning for the first time since last September middle. Great praise to the kind and preserving Father, who has given me health and strength enough for it.

April 20. — The body feels the pressure of daily toil, and the vigor of early life is wanting. It is a drag on the physical man, in all these days, to accomplish the work of life. But it is best to work.

May 3. — Lib's birthday, — threescore. Thank God that she is in so good health, and has such good prospect of added years. She will outlive me, probably, by a good many years, but heaven re-unites.

On this day he accompanied a beautiful gift with the following poem : —

" For what is your life? It is even a vapor that appeareth for a little time, and then vanisheth away." — JAS. iv. 14.

> Sixty years of so-called vapor
>   Gone from life's mysterious mist;
> Six decades of that strange fog-bank —
>   One more such completes the list.
>
> Suddenly, on life's horizon,
>   Hung a cloud unseen before ;
> Suddenly, on death's horizon,
>   Comes a cloud soon seen no more.
>
> Sometimes like the cloud on Sinai,
>   With its tempest, fire, and smoke;
> Sometimes like the veil of darkness,
>   That on wondrous Calvary broke ;
>
> Always like the desert pillar,
>   Israel's guide by day or night,
> Hallowed by the living Presence,
>   Shedding forth his inner light ;
>
> Sometimes like Elijah's cloudlet,
>   Token of the blessed rain,
> That should fill the empty fountains,
>   And refresh the thirsty plain ;
>
> Sometimes, in the revelations
>   Of the soul's diviner mood,
> Like the cloud of glory covering
>   The transfigured Son of God.

> When thy cloud-life nears dissolving,
> Sailing, sailing towards the west,
> May it melt, 'mid evening splendors,
> Into heaven's eternal rest.

May 17. — My birthday. Thanks be to God for fifty-nine years of his ceaseless love, and unvaried forbearance, and abundant temporal and spiritual gifts; for home, and friends, and friendships! Lord, make the remainder rich with love to thee.

On the seventh day of June we enjoyed the communion service in our old Methodist Episcopal Church, — that church hallowed by the ministrations of Fisk and Olin, and where hundreds of faithful ones, since taken home, had bowed to "drink the wine and break the bread." I shall never forget the thought that crowded into my mind, as we knelt side by side at the altar: "You will no more together celebrate your Lord's death '*till He come.*'"

The following Saturday morning has this note in his diary: "Karl's birthday, and he is home to enjoy it with us. Thanks be to God, who has spared him and us till now. It is marked by the burning of the Methodist Church, which burned this morning. Now for a new one."

His sorrow at the fire was less marked than might have been expected, for he had long felt that the cause of God and of Methodism was suffering from this unattractive place of worship. He said, a little time before, when money was being expended to rejuvenate it somewhat, "We ought to build a new one, but we never shall unless the Lord burns this old one down." Evidently he had a half belief, at least, that in this way God had indeed come to rescue his own cause. At once he was full of zeal, in his prayers and plans, for rebuilding the walls of Zion, and of regrets that he had not strength to devote to earnest work for it.

CHAPTER XI.

ALUMNI MEETING AT TILTON.—EXTRACTS FROM POEM.

EARLY in this year he had been solicited to write a poem to deliver at the forty-first alumni gathering at the old seminary where he spent the first eight years after graduation. He had consented conditionally, and during the spring months, little by little, as his strength would allow, he had written it. As the time approached, his friends felt assured that it was too perilous an undertaking. But his friendships were the dearest things in life, and he longed to meet the old students and professors once again. He wanted to go to that first home where he began domestic life, and the life of teaching that he had continued for thirty-three years, and give it a final blessing and farewell. He pleaded that, instead of injuring, he thought the journey, carefully taken, would be such a break in the fatigues of examination and commencement, that it would prove favorable. Accordingly, with the utmost care, the journey was made. The old first home was open to receive us. Though our Father had taken thence to himself the honored one, who, in former days, was our kind and genial host, yet the warmest welcome and tenderest ministrations were given to the returning invalid. Carefully carried to the Seminary Hall, he took his place on the platform, and, with the determination almost of desperation, he stood an hour before his audience, making the last public literary effort of his life. Below are a few extracts from the poem, which was entitled —

THE SCHOOL OF LIFE.

Some teachers never die. Kearsarge,
That yonder keeps its solemn charge,
Lifts its bald head and furrowed brow,
Looks calmly on the valleys now
As when the centuries had their birth,
And God from chaos spoke the earth.
Over the vales and streams below,
Where generations come and go,
It stretches forth its hand benign,
Utters its lessons all divine,
Echoes God's voice, tells men to be
Strong as the hills, as breezes free ;
O'er low-born grovelling to rise,
Like mountain heights to meet the skies.

And Winnipiseogee's healthful stream,
Born in broad waters, where the gleam
Of mountain sunsets gilds the wave
That ripples low, or leaps to lave
The island's green and grassy shore —
How, rushing seaward evermore,
It tells us of the stream of time,
The eternal sea, in rippling rhyme ;
Of constancy and quiet power,
And cheerful labor every hour !

Nor mount and stream alone : the sky
That arches earth, the fiery eye
Of day, the tender orb of night,
The twinkling worlds of starry light, —
Each from its magisterial seat
Speaks its own language, clear, replete
With wisdom for the dullest soul
That humbly aims for wisdom's goal.

So, when the years their work have wrought, —
Buried the teacher and the taught,

Reared watching tombstones o'er the grave
Where sighing pines and cypress wave,
Wrinkled fair brows, silvered the head,
Given nimble feet a tottering tread,
Set on the noblest mould of clay
The seal of time, death, and decay, —
Standing where once, in other years,
Life knew its cares and hopes and fears;
'Mid scenes the same, yet not the same,
Old and yet new, except in name;
'Tis sweet, when memory wakes the past,
Revives the dreams that could not last,
When voiceless shadows fill the place
That living forms were wont to grace,
To find some things that ne'er grow old,
That tell the tales they've always told.
That far-off mount and stream near by
Tell us "*some* teachers never die."

. . . .

Alas that the Christian home in its ideal
Should be so far distant from home in the real!
Let man make the home what his Maker designed it,
And for making the man it leaves all schools behind it.
The house may be palace or hovel, no matter;
The table-ware, silver or worn wooden platter;
The walls, grimed with smoke, of rude logs put together,
Or solid of marble, and proof against weather;
The windows of holes, and the latch-string of leather,
The lawn but a sand-heap, the stable a tether;
Or windows and doors of glass heavily plated,
And lawn just a paradise newly created:
Not these make the home, neither place nor surrounding,
But warm and true hearts, in affection abounding.
Yet outward adornment will match with the inner,
Just as virtue inside is not outside a sinner;
And beauty without will give instant impression
What kind of a home sits in inward possession.

The dooryard, well kept with its violets and roses,
The spirit and temper within well discloses.
There love is enthroned, with authority blended,
By firmness and patience and such like attended.
The child renders ready and willing obedience
When the wish of the parent requires his allegiance;
And varied amusement, good music, good reading,
With thousand amenities, mutual love breeding,
Make home of all places the sweetest in pleasure,
With dividends richer than mines of hid treasure,
While a spirit divine as the true breath of heaven
Takes God and his Word as the household's pure leaven.

. . . .

Let this darksome picture pass, and give brighter scenes a chance.
On the panoramic field let the common school advance.
From the turmoil of the town, with its atmosphere of death,
Let us drink the draughts of life in the country's wholesome breath.
Take a glance at the foundation of a free and happy state, —
The humble rustic schoolhouse, insignificant yet great.
On the slope beyond the village, or, if village there be none,
On the grass-plat at the cross-roads, or by mossy ledge of stone,
At the bottom of the hillside where the brook comes tumbling down,
And the raspberry-canes with blushing fruit the pasture hillocks crown,
By the pond where leaps the trout, and the dripping swallow flies,
And among the smooth green pads the cradled lily lies, —
On the hill and in the vale, everywhere through all the land,
These humble, mighty schoolrooms with their hidden forces stand.
Take a glance within the room, with its walls of wood or brick,
Where some honest man or maiden wields the sceptre and the stick;
Where cheerful childhood faces greet the teacher's kindly look,
As they tell the lessons over they have gathered from the book.
Here the country's future freemen learn what freemen ought to know,
And reveal the lines of promise which the coming years will show.
Yonder bench supports a statesman, now on ardent study bent;
This, a judge, who'll wear the ermine; that, a future president;

Or, since all can't be presidents, nor wear a judge's wig,
They will at least be qualified, though really not so big.
And if the farm, the forge, the mill, shall be their after sphere,
They'll tell the tale with pride, no doubt, that they were tutored
    here.

. . . .

   Turn we now another leaf
   Of these picture-pages brief.
   'Twill occasion no surprise
   If the college meet your eyes.
   Goal of many a boyish dream,
   Goal of many a thought the theme;
   To imagination's eye
   Clothed with awful majesty,
   Like to Delos' sacred shrine
   With its oracle divine.
   Here grave doctors sit in state,
   Dropping wisdom in debate;
   Learned professors stuffed with lore,
   All the ancients knew, and more;
   Libraries, whose ivied walls
   Gather in their ample halls
   Alcoves piled with ponderous tome,
   Shrining ancient Greece and Rome;
   Or in far less dusty page
   Wise words from the modern sage.
   Thus to Fancy's distant view
   Men and things wear golden hue,
   And to young Ambition's dream
   Common things superior seem.
   But college walls are only walls,
   College halls like other halls.
   Men who tread on college ground,
   When you know them, will be found
   Just like men of common mould, —
   Some of putty, some of gold.
   Think not that the college mill
   Grinds out wise men, will or nill,

Nor that every grist contains
Quite the maximum of brains.
What the hopper first receives,
That the whirling mill-stone gives;
'Tisn't in the college plan
That mere grinding *makes* the man.
Let the lazy dude go in, —
Hat and cane and bosom-pin;
If he stand the wear and tear
Of the grinding process there,
He'll come out as he went in, —
Hat and cane and bosom-pin.

. . . . . .

Christian faith and Christian prayer,
Christian sacrifice and care,
Holy fire the anointing chrism,
Holy tears the rich baptism,
Founded colleges and schools,
Made them freedom's sacred tools,
Laid their corner-stones in truth,
Fills them with our noble youth,
Sends these, trained in heart and mind,
Forth, a blessing to mankind,
Trained in heart with pious care
By the frequent voice of prayer
Daily heard at common shrine,
Daily honoring Power Divine.
Thus, if the good the bad outweighs,
Give the whole due meed of praise.
Shall a few wrecks on the shore
Furl all sails forevermore?
Shall some drones with lazy feet
Poison all the honey sweet?
If bad men good things abuse,
Shall good men have none to use?
Schools of learning are the stream
Which the desert wastes redeem;

Or the dew and grateful rain,
Fertilizing all the plain.
Lo! their fruitage everywhere
Touching us like balmy air;
Light diffused in myriad homes,
Light condensed in myriad tomes;
Sweetening leaven of Church and State,
Comforter of small and great;
Rills of life from heavenly sources,
Blessing all in all their courses.
Palsied be the recreant arm —
Let all good men take the alarm —
That would break the holy tie
Linking them to God on high,
From their walls the Bible tear,
Hush therein the voice of prayer !
But, religion's handmaid mild,
As they are religion's child,
Let the child and mother, too,
Fight the peaceful battle through,
Till the King of peace shall reign
Over land and stream and main.

. . . .

Somewhere in life's curriculum,
Ordained by Him who knows us best,
Sorrow, dark-browed, unbars her room,
And bids us follow her behest.
We dread to cross that threshold drear,
Our feet reluctant tread her halls,
Hung with the drapery of fear,
Where every sight and sound appals.
The furniture adds more dismay,
The shroud, the casket, and the pall,
The hearse with raven plumes that play
And nod their grim adieus to all.
Groans are the music echoing down
From brazen roof and walls of art ;

Tears are the tide of sorrow's moan, —
The blood-drops of a broken heart.
Patience is oft the lesson set,
And Pain the teacher strong and stern;
While Woe bids Pride its pride forget,
And Grief bids Joy her tasks to learn.
What form is that, grim, gaunt, and pale,
We gaze upon with bated breath,
Whose shadow wakes a smothered wail?
It is the dreaded teacher, Death.
Hush! he has hurled his fatal dart:
What words can agony employ?
What still the mother's bursting heart?
O God! it was my only boy.
Hush! still that form relentless speeds,
Nor heeds the look that pleads though mute:
That stroke puts on a widow's weeds,
And orphaned children are its fruit.
Hush! still glides on that stealthy tread,
While pallor blanches every cheek;
Beauty and strength are with the dead;
Eyes look the grief they cannot speak.
In yonder churchyard, 'mid its graves,
Sad Meditation turns her feet,
Where willows weep and cypress waves,
And Sorrow rears her chosen seat.
Hard problems, and hard lessons too,
Beyond the skill of human ken,
Affliction sets for me and you,
And all the living sons of men.
Leave them unsolved. No mortal can
Explain the things with mystery rife;
Wait for the Master's voice, "I am
The resurrection and the life."

. .   .   .

Some teachers never die. Kearsarge,
That yonder keeps his silent charge,

And Winnipiseogee's cheerful roar
Adown its slant and rocky floor,
Like yonder starry heavens do tell
His glory and his work full well.
Day unto day hath voice for man,
Night unto night reveals his plan;
Their line encircles all the earth,
Their voice wherever man has birth;
His works in earth or heaven make known
What the eternal God hath done,
Nor cease until this goodly frame
Shall vanish in the final flame.
Are breathless things more deathless than
The living soul — immortal man?
More true, 'some teachers never die,'
Of mount and stream and starry sky,
Than him whose life is God's own breath,
Made to be victor over death?
Is Barrows dead? Nay, rather, shrined
In countless throbbing hearts, that bind
The laurel wreath upon his head;
Pilgrims that oft in memory tread
Where sighing pines their watches keep
Above his *body's* dreamless sleep.
As pulses of the viewless light,
That ceaseless chase the flying night,
His words of eloquence sublime
Shall live and work till latest time.
And when the voice on sea and shore
Proclaims that time shall be no more,
The guerdon of his work shall be
A twofold immortality.

   And Latimer, the noble-souled,
With learning's princes high enrolled,
Strong in his gentleness, and great
In gifts to bless or Church or State, —
Has that fine soul forever fled
To Auburn, city of the dead?

Lives he not yet, lives he not long,
In human hearts, on human tongue?
Will not his words from wisdom's seat,
The future generations greet,
Caught up like echoes far away,
To linger till the eternal day?

. . . .

Life's varied schools and discipline
Are all ordained by Power Divine.
He built the earth, and spread the sea,
And hung the starry canopy;
A schoolroom for the human race,
Where each should take his proper place,
Learners in all of earthly lore
That fits us for an earthly shore.
Then the great Teacher came to show
What mortal knowledge could not know;
To say to all men, 'Learn of me
The lore of immortality.'
And some day, on his cloudy throne,
He'll come to number up his own,
To place them in the school on high,
Where pupils also never die.
That all this company be there,
Shall be your humble poet's prayer."

CHAPTER XII.

EXAMINATIONS AND COMMENCEMENT. — PROFESSOR EMERITUS. — INCREASING WEAKNESS. — THE LORD'S LEADING. — MUSIC.

HAVING thus accomplished his purpose, he returned to Middletown the following day. June 19, he wrote: "Home again! How sweet the word! The Lord has given me strength thus far. Now for another hard day. But 'as thy days, so shall thy strength be.' Lord, help me to take the promise."

The three examinations he would have had on three successive days, must be, from his absence, crowded into this one. But though his kind colleagues begged to relieve him of the work, he said, "No: I have finished my year thus far, I will not fail at the end."

He attended the three examinations in college, finished computing the standing of his classes, and passed in his report, as was his custom at the close of every term. He examined the proof of the "Obituary Record of the Alumni of the University," which he had prepared, — a work he had done annually since 1863; and when all was accomplished, then he meant to rest. Saturday morning, the 20th, he wrote: "Sustained to do the necessary work of yesterday, and apparently no worse for it. To-day I hope to rest. Oh, how good the word seems! It seems to me I never knew what it was to be tired till now." Still he hoped that the vacation would so recruit him that he might be able to take at least as much and perhaps more work the next year than he had done in the last. But the record in his diary on the 24th of the same month is as follows: —

"Who knoweth what a day may bring forth? I am suddenly made professor emeritus, without work, on half pay. It is probably the wisest course, and the best for me. So the Lord's will be done, and may I be the better."

The evening before, as he returned exhausted from a ride to the society receptions, he found awaiting him two of the trustees of the college, who announced to him the above fact. Though he received it with apparent calmness, it was like an unexpected thunderbolt. "Why," said he when they left, "what are we to do? I am without any warning thrown out of my work, and my means of support half cut off." — I said, "We must live on the half, then." — "We cannot do it," said he, "it is impossible. We have never, since we kept house, lived on so little as that, and with the great increase of expense resulting from my sickness it is impossible. And what does it all mean?" he continued. "It indicates very plainly what others think of my case. Evidently, in their opinion, my life-work is done." For a few days the cloud was heavy upon him. Then he began to see the silver lining, and to see God out of the thick darkness. He said, "After all, it is all of the Lord. I do not want to remain in my place in college to be a hinderance to its prosperity. Others probably understand better than I can, what is best in this matter. So, though I did want to stand at my post as long as possible, probably it is better thus. The trustees are under no legal obligation to give me any thing. A half loaf is far better than none." And so his prayers were changed to praises, and he repeatedly expressed afterward his belief that the hand of the Lord was in it all.

He attended a part of the exercises of commencement day, greeted with pleasure many old friends, and enjoyed heartily the guests in his home, especially his old-time friends Professor H. B. Lane and wife. It was the chair of the genial and generous Professor Lane that he took on first coming to his work in Wesleyan, and he expressed great gratification that he was able to entertain them in his home once more. When all was over, and the stimulus of the yearly festival gone, he began to realize more fully his weakness. He and Professor Westgate had a few weeks before engaged rooms for themselves and families for a few weeks in a house together at the Adirondacks. Both found the project must be abandoned. The news of Professor Westgate's death reached him on July 29, and was a great surprise and shock. "I had no idea," said he, "that he was so far gone. He is at rest, and is to be envied for his calm repose." Only a day later, Professor J. C. Burke was also laid away to rest. Mr. Harrington was very desirous to attend both these burial-services, but reluctantly gave it up, as his strength was quite unequal to the strain upon his emotions. So close together these two whom he admired and loved were taken home! He said, "The fighting for life and health goes on, but it seems sometimes a useless warfare. Death marches on. The influential and wealthy do not escape. The young and strong are seized."

Time unoccupied began to be burdensome, and the heat of summer was exceedingly oppressive to his weakness. He said, "My work must be to endure, chiefly, yet something useful and helpful may be done to somebody."

A visit from his youngest sister greatly relieved the tediousness of two or three weeks. The hours were filled with delightful communion, and a union of faith and prayer. "What would the world be," said he, "without the loves and charities of men? It is one of God's richest bestowments to give us kind friends." When she left he noted it in his diary, adding, "It is not very likely I shall ever see her again in this world. We have had a pleasant visit, and I am thankful for having had her with us for a while."

On the morning of Aug. 10, he wrote in his diary: "Thirty-three years ago to-day! How different the situation! What a world of good things has been the outcome of that day! The years of the generation have been full of blessing."

We talked that day of all the way God had led us; and he exclaimed, "If ever a man had cause for gratitude to God for thirty-three years of blessedness, I am he." I answered, "We have had a great many good times together." — "Oh," said he, "they have been all good; they have been constantly growing better, and these last times are the very best of the whole."

His confidence in the special care and leading of Divine Providence was unwavering, and during the last years was constantly increasing. During these summer and autumn months, he spent much time in his hammock in the grove in the rear of his home, either in conversation, reading, or listening to reading. One day he said, "Bring out the old letter-box, and let us look over our past a little." For several days thereafter, we found this a pleasant pastime. Selecting here and there different epochs in our history, we called up the circumstances, and remembered the questionings and the motives that had influenced our course, and the helplessness with which we had asked God's guidance; and here now, standing on the elevation of experience, we could see plainly the wonderful pillar of cloud by day, and of fire by night, that in all the years had safely led us on. Again and again he exclaimed, "I can account for it in no other way. It was the hand of God." And this was no cold theory to him. God's presence and God's love and God's especial care were living realities. This little poem written on the night of Dec. 31, 1880, was the expression of his sincerest faith : —

THE LORD'S LEADING.

"And thou shalt remember all the way which the Lord thy God led thee."
— DEUT. viii. 2.

  Sitting by the whitening embers
   Of the shivering, dying year,
  Ah ! how well my soul remembers
   All the way he led me here.

  Sheltered by the Rock of Ages,
   By Siloa's healthful tide,
  Where no stormy tempest rages,
   He hath led me by his side.

  In the mines where God's hid treasure
   Gleams in galleries of gold,
  'Mid the wealth of his good pleasure,
   He hath made my path unfold.

Battling in the billowy sweetness
  Of his mercy's ocean store,
I had drowned, o'erwhelmed with riches;
  But he led me to the shore.

When the path grew dark with sorrow,
  Still I held his loving hand;
And he gave a brighter morrow,
  Brought me to a pleasant land.

Every step my Lord hath led me,
  Through the swiftly circling year;
All the way his bounty fed me,
  Soothed my sadness, calmed my fear.

Thankful, him my soul remembers,
  Sitting by the hearthstone here,
Where the slowly whitening embers
  Mark the shivering, dying year.

One of these days he spoke of the probability that he could not remain with me much longer. I said, "If I could go with you, I would be satisfied to have it so." — "Yes, we would love to go together," he answered; "but that would make it too sad for Karl. I should like to live to see him happy in a home of his own. I cannot expect it; but I want you to live to encourage and help him until he has his own family, and is well established in life." His diary of Aug. 22 says, "Karl left us this morning for Wilbraham. It seems hard to be without him; but the best thing for him is to go out alone, and battle with the world. God bless him with the indwelling Spirit!"

The loneliness of the following week was relieved by a visit from his only brother. Lying in his hammock while his brother sat by, they talked of their boyhood and youth; and many a time the old trees above them echoed their hearty laughter as they recalled the sports and freaks, adventures and escapes, of those early days. Then they spun the thread on into manhood; and their voices grew solemn and tender, as they mingled their words of Christian faith, and strengthened each other with their firm, glad hope of an immortality together.

Aug. 27 he wrote in the diary: "Leonard left us last night. The visit has been a very pleasant one. Is it the last?" So it proved.

That day he seated himself at the organ, and ran over the keys for some time, then scribbled a bit. Being asked, "What are you doing?" he laughed, and said, "Listen, and I'll show you." Then he played and sang to a tune he had just made the following words: —

> "Lord, for to-morrow and its needs,
>   I do not pray;
> Keep me, my God, from stain of sin
>   Just for to-day.
>
> "Let me both diligently work,
>   And duly pray;
> Let me be kind in word and deed,
>   Just for to-day.
>
> "So for to-morrow and its needs,
>   I do not pray;
> But keep me, guide me, love me, Lord,
>   Just for to-day."

His brother-in-law had sent him the hymn to set to music, a few weeks earlier; and he had replied he was too weak to attempt it. But now it relieved the sadness of the recent departure. Twice afterward, he went to the organ, and sang and played the same thing. The sentiment was a helpful one in his condition, and he enjoyed it. Since his boyhood he had frequently practised the composition of music, and was in the habit of cutting from papers bits of poetry that especially pleased him, and adapting them to song. Dr. Warren's "Homeward Bound" was thus brought into use. He wrote the music while teaching at Sanbornton Bridge, and sang it often in social meetings. One of his pupils asked for a copy of it, which he wrote for her. During vacation she attended camp-meeting, and sang it. It was quickly caught up by the musical brother Dadmun, and soon came out in a volume of his, but with such change in arrangement that the author never afterward enjoyed singing it, except alone.

"The Lord will provide" was another written in the same way; and in his last diary were left several little stray poems, awaiting his leisure to put them to music. Many songs he sang at funerals were in music that had never been written, but lived only in his own soul of melody.

CHAPTER XIII.

FAILING PHYSICAL AND INCREASING SPIRITUAL STRENGTH. — —"BORDER-LAND." — VISITS. — LETTERS. — KINDNESS OF FRIENDS. — PREACHING. — HEART-SEARCHINGS. — BISHOP FOSS. — DAY OF PRAYER. — NIGHT-EXPERIENCES.

ONE more entry in Mr. Harrington's diary, which he had kept with scarcely an omission of a day, except in sickness, for nearly a third of a century, and the last he ever wrote, was made on Aug. 31 : " So ends the month, and the summer. What a change it has brought to many ! For me, the slow decline, and nearing steps of death. Yet the Lord is in it all. I will praise him." During that week there had come a sudden failing of strength, that was very marked. He thought the end was rapidly approaching, and with this belief came a great uplifting of spirit. On Sunday, at the hour for church service, I read to him, as was my custom, portions of Scripture, and other religious works of his own selection. "Read me, to-day," said he, "the fourteenth chapter of John." As I read, he continually interrupted me with comments and praises, and tears of joy. When I reached the twenty-seventh verse, he said, " Oh, stop there ! I can't bear any more. That verse fills me *full, full*. Glory to God !" For an hour he continued in an ecstasy of joy ; and for days thereafter he was full of joyous anticipations, thinking himself greatly favored to be so near the beautiful home above. One morning he exclaimed, "I will praise the Lord at all times; his praise shall continually be in my mouth." Then added, "I have no dread of death, but a calm rest in the Lord. I do not think it is stupor, but it is what Dr. Ladd used to call it, *great peace;* a wonderful comfort. I have no doubts, no fears, no dreads. I am in my Father's hands. I have such a wonderful victory over the temptations that all my life have been a curse to me. It seems to me now, if I could go back, it would be so easy to put them all under my feet."

Some one mentioned to him the little poem he had written entitled "The Border-Land." He answered, "The best thing about that is, it is all my own present experience."

> On the solemn border standing
>   Of the land unseen, unknown,
> 'Neath Death's shadow, hushed I listen
>   For the hymns around the throne.
> Doubts and fears around me thronging
>   Swell the load of daily care:
> Who shall satisfy my longing?
>   Who my burdens help to bear?
>
> Jesus comes; his gentle finger
>   Lifts the load, and it is gone;
> Jesus comes; where shadows linger,
>   Lo! the purpling of the morn;
> And when trembling fear comes o'er me,
>   When 'mid doubts I scarce can pray,
> If the Master stand before me,
>   Doubts and fears all melt away.
>
> When my guilty soul sinks under
>   All the crushing weight of sin,
> Jesus comes; O joy and wonder!
>   Strength and hope are back again.

> He gives victory in my conflict;
> He from sorrow sends release;
> When the gathering storm is darkest,
> Jesus lifts the bow of peace.

One of the alumni came to call on his former teacher; and in reply to questions, Professor Harrington answered, "My body is pretty weak, but it is well with my soul. Cooper, I am just as happy as I can be." He was not only happy in his religion now, but he was happy in every thing, entering into all the topics of the day with pleasure.

During the months of September and October he received visits from his eldest sister, his brother's wife, and from a nephew who bore his name, and possessed very nearly his own voice for singing. With great delight, Mr. Harrington would lie on the lounge, selecting song after song of his favorites, and listen to their rendering. Kindred ties were especially sacred to him. In a letter dictated to his sister, after her departure, he says, "May the Lord bless your soul and body, and give you health and peace; and every member of your family be included! There is nothing I desire more for my kindred, whom I love, than that they be kept in the love of God, and have an abiding hope of eternal life. Next to that, I wish them such worldly prosperity as will make them comfortable in this life, and able to do good as they have opportunity. My thoughts run to you and to your interests very often. I desire the health especially of the household, and look in upon you in imagination, and follow you in your daily life. I carry along in my thoughts, and frequently recur with gratitude to, the loving attentions and kindness that you have so often shown us, and hope the Lord may reward you."

In another letter, after speaking of the pleasure the visits had given him, he said, "So all the blessings of life show the exceeding mercies of God to make affliction light, and the burden of sickness less heavy to bear. And mightier than all, for help and support, are the everlasting arms that hold me constantly in their loving embrace. God lets me have a clear light and a confident trust. I cannot give you the details of my experience beyond this. My health does not vary, that is, apparently, from day to day. What the invisible progress of the disease is working, time only will tell; and that I await without fear or anxiety."

One Sunday he asked to hear Dr. Spear's article on "The Heavenly Home," found in the "Independent" of Oct. 1, 1885.

After we had expressed our mutual adoption of its sentiments, he said, "I am so glad that this is the faith of us both, that we can rest in the Bible-promises, and that they are so real to us. It is not God's plan to let husband and wife go over the river of death together, but we can go together to its edge; and I can't help believing that there will be *some little link* that will hold when we are in the two worlds. And the separation will be short, — *oh, so short!*" Then, after a little, he added, "I do hope I shall not get impatient. I hope I shall be willing to wait all God's time. Whether it is only a week, or I have to suffer on for months, it is all right, *all right*. And I do hope I may be able to make God's will my will, — to wait patiently." I said, "Would you really rather go now, than to wait any longer?" — "If it were God's will, — yes, *oh, yes!*" he answered. Then, looking up, he said, "Only for the *separations*, I would be glad to go home now. It will be hard to leave you and Karl, — I cannot think of that, — but that must come, and it will make but little difference when. A short separation, and then a whole eternity together."

I asked if he thought he was growing weaker.

"Sometimes I do," said he; "especially yesterday and to-day. I am *so tired!*" Once he said, "Oh, this dreadful cough is so tiresome !" then immediately checked himself, and added, "But it is God's will, and so it is my will."

During the following two or three weeks his strength rallied again considerable. As I finished his toilet one morning, he said, " How much longer will you have to do all this for me?— " How much longer shall I have the privilege?" said I. "But if I should live on and on for months?" he said. "For years I would be happy in doing it, only for the grief of seeing you suffer," I answered. He smiled, and said, "Well, I am thankful that I do not have to suffer very seriously. If it were not for this short breath, I could do considerable; with this, I can't do any thing; but when I lie quiet I suffer comparatively little, and no acute pain. I ought to be so thankful ! " I spoke of the joy of having him here, and said if I should allow my mind to dwell on his going away, I could not care for him as he needed. "Oh, do not do that: there is no need to anticipate sorrow," said he. "Let us enjoy each other while we can. Let us live in the present 'just for to-day.'" Then, referring to his exultant joy a few weeks before, when he thought he was going very soon, he said, " I do not need that now; but I have what I do need, — grace of patience to wait. Just the grace needed will come just when and as we need it." I said, "I am glad you do not wear an unhappy or distressed face, as many sick ones do." He replied, "I have too much confidence in God's constant and minute care over me, to feel unhappy at any thing he does."

He especially enjoyed the sacrament of the Lord's Supper. I think he had the fulness of that experience expressed by Dr. Cuyler in the words, "Sometimes at the Lord's table, Jesus comes into the soul just as he did into that upper chamber where the disciples were assembled." On the first day of November, he said, "As we cannot go to communion in the church to-day, we must do the best we can to get the same blessings at home. Read the fifty-first Psalm. That is such a full confession of sin, and contrite humbling of soul, it seems to me especially appropriate for us all at such a time." His responses to it indicated his own contrition of spirit before God. Then he asked for some of his favorite hymns, — "There's a wideness in God's mercy." Oh, with what pathos he repeated the lines, —

"And the heart of the Eternal
Is most *wonderfully* kind!"

He greatly delighted in the reading of the Psalms. "How full they are," said he, "of a settled, unwavering confidence in God! David seems not to have had a shadow of a doubt of the reality and character of the Creator. Read me Lucy's Psalm," — referring to the 121st, which a friend had quoted in a conversation with him. After the reading, he said, "Now, see if I can repeat it right." And having done so, he exclaimed, "*Oh, yes! my* help cometh from the Lord." He called for several others, and finally said, "Now read me some of the short ones, near the end of the book, that are all full of praise." And his own praises were very fervently added. He talked much of the "peace of God," and tried to express what "the peace of God that passeth all understanding" was to him. He finally summed it up by: "'It is Christ with us and Christ in us.' As I lay coughing last night," he continued, "I thought, 'I know now what the apostle meant by "joy unspeakable."' I used to wonder if I should ever understand it: now I think I do. I know what it is. Praise the Lord!"

He was exceedingly appreciative of any acts of kindness received, and these acts were continually multiplied by all about us.

When his strength so suddenly failed the last of August, it became exceedingly difficult for him to go up-stairs, and he could only do so by leaning very heavily with both hands, and resting on each stair. Mr. Merrill, who had taken his work in the Latin department, came often to consult him, and cheer him with reports from his classes. On the evening of Sept. 3, he proposed to help him up-stairs, saying, "I can carry you up, professor, in my arms." Mr. Harrington laughed at the idea as preposterous; but his friend persisted, and with much pleading was finally allowed to try it. I shall never forget the look of relief and delight as he was placed safely in the chair in his chamber, and saw that the dreaded task was spared him. Every night afterward, this great kindness was shown him. Tutor White, the son of a dear college classmate, begged the privilege of sharing in this labor of love; and, soon afterward, he began to come also each morning about eleven o'clock to take him down to the parlor.

And so many weary months, that must otherwise have been spent shut in a sick-chamber, were made far more cheerful and happy in the family parlor, where he enjoyed calls of neighbors and friends, and interested himself in all the topics of the household and city.

On Sunday, Nov. 15, after Mr. White left him on the lounge, he burst into tears; and when asked the cause, he said, " I was thinking of the goodness of God. Every thing about me is so pleasant, so comforting; I have been brought down-stairs so safely, so easily; my swollen limb is a little better, and every thing tells of God's wonderful kindness." I answered, " We have not half found out his goodness yet." — " *Half* learned it! Talk of *half* finding out an *unfathomable fact!* " he exclaimed. I read the 103d Psalm. Said he, " I believe that, and the 23d, and 121st, and 27th, are the ones I like a little the best." Then, with emphasis, he added the 91st, and said, " I guess we shall find a good many more we shall want to class with these."

On Monday he inquired about the services of the preceding day, then compared his Sundays now and formerly. He said, " I used to feel it a terrible cross to preach in College Chapel. I did not have at all the assurance that it was my duty to do so, for I always questioned if it were not a disadvantage to the students. It seemed to me to give them an indolent, irresponsible church-life. Then I dreaded every effort I made there, you cannot conceive how severely; partly because I doubted the wisdom of the whole plan; partly because my audience came to hear me by compulsion; especially because I disliked to be pitted against some others who had been pastors for years, and had a quantity of sermons ready, so they could preach with comparatively little effort. But perhaps that was just the discipline the Lord saw I needed. I know I did struggle hard against that temptation, — as I presume now it was. I said to myself, 'It is none of your business; you have no right to make your personal success any motive in your Christian work. All pride, and envy, and ambition, should be entirely overcome in this matter.' I know I used to pray a good deal over every sermon. Especially I remember the sermon on prayer. I felt a great burden on that subject, and I begged God to help me speak the truth."

During the month of December he continually lost flesh and strength, though his appetite and digestion were both good. At some times he would talk quite hopefully of being able to preach and sing again. On other days he would talk of the better land, and rejoice in anticipation of it. He was constantly cheerful and often quite merry, amusing himself in all the little occurrences of the times. He dictated a letter on Dec. 5, commencing as follows: "We have just finished, Lib and I, our dinner-duet, consisting, by the programme, of common and sweet potatoes, beefsteak, and celery for a relish. There were two solo parts; Lib's was bread and butter, and mine onions. The second part of the programme was pumpkin-pie and apples. The performance was very successful, and no doubt we shall be called upon to repeat the programme.

"Now I am stretched on the lounge — which I occupy much of the time — digesting my dinner, coughing at intervals, and dictating this epistle. It is a gloomy day out of doors, but inside there is comfort; not only in the supply of our wants, and in the providential surroundings, but in the communion of two that have long been one, and whom time and growing age, and the tests of these later days, weld together in a more inseparable union. And when you add to these the 'peace of God that passeth all understanding,' what more could we ask to sweeten our daily joys? And yet other things do enhance the enjoyments of our life. We have just proved it in the vacation visit of Karl and Carrie, who brought the light of young hearts to cheer and stir us up." — I queried a bit here as to the correctness of his rhetoric, when he said, "Oh, you wait; I shall make that all right," and immediately added, "as a lamp carried into an old closet stirs up the old beetles, and bugs, and spiders, from their lairs, and sets them to taking healthy exercise."

At this time he was unable to bear his own weight, and only sat up two or three hours a day. As the month progressed, he began to suffer more from short breath, and many days his fever was very high. Still his energy of spirit did not forsake him. Several times during the month he rode for an hour in the bracing air, and returned refreshed. On Saturday, the 29th, he went out for the last time. He was driven to the new church building, where he was interested in its progress and proportions. The whole ride was pleasing, and gave him subject for recreative thought some days. Several times afterward he proposed riding, but failed to obtain his physician's approval. His cough increased, and during the nights was especially severe. Early in January, he called out once, about midnight, "Who is it that shall ascend into the hill of the Lord? *Who* shall stand in his holy place?" I replied, "He that hath clean hands and a pure heart." — " What else?" said he, "I want to apply the whole test to myself." I continued, "Who hath not lifted up his soul unto vanity, nor sworn deceitfully." — "Yes, '*sworn deceitfully*,'" said he : "are you sure I have not done that?" — "Why, of all things, *yes*, I am sure you never swore deceitfully." — "But," said he, "I want to be very sure. You remember I have one share in the ———— stock company; I did not put it into my tax-list." — "Why should you?" said I. "It is not worth a penny, has brought you no interest for years, and probably never will be of any value to you." — "Ah! that makes no difference," he said; "the question is, does the law require me to report it? I did not think of it when I made out my list, and I do not suppose it should be reckoned, because as a corporation it pays taxes in another State. But I want you to write to Homer," — a brother-in-law, — "and ask if by any law of Connecticut or New York that ought to be put in my tax-list." When the reply came assuring him there was none, he said, "Well, that is settled; I don't know of any thing else I have not attended to correctly." He talked very frequently, and with perfect freedom, of the changes that were coming to us. He made all arrangements possible for the future comfort of his family; he gave advice on many little matters that it seemed marvellous he should remember in the midst of his suffering. He received calls during all this month from all the friends who came. It was a great pleasure to him to see them. And especially he enjoyed the visits of those who conversed freely with him of mutual Christian experience; and expressed much surprise that the majority of Christians, and even Christian ministers, did not talk more of their own religious experience.

He said, one day, as I went into his room, "I have some comfort in the promise you read me this morning, 'He who hath begun a good work in you will perform it until the day of the Lord Jesus.' I am sure *I* have begun no good work, but I am sure a good work has been begun in me, for I know that something has helped me to overcome the carnal nature; and I don't believe He who has begun it will leave it unfinished."

"Read me some of the 119th Psalm," said he; "that gets neglected because it is so long." After the reading of that, he said, "Now read the hymn 'Abide with me.'" When the hymn was ended, he repeated, with much emphasis and emotion, all of the last stanza, and added, "*He will.* I am sure he *will.*" This hymn he asked for very often, and often repeated, and more than once sang it in the night, once when he was fast asleep. Also, once during sleep he sang clearly, —

> "Jesus, my all, to heaven is gone,
> He whom I fix my hopes upon;
> His track I see, and I'll pursue
> The narrow way till him I view."

Sunday, Jan. 24, he spent in his chamber, and most of the day in bed. In the afternoon Bishop Foss, who came to the city the preceding evening, called to see him. The hour was one of the most delightful to him of all his sickness. The bishop had been down to the gates of death, and he knew just how to touch the chords of heavenly comfort that would vibrate harmoniously in that place. They compared their experiences, and neither needed to explain. The fewest words were understood. Heart answered heart, as they talked of the revelations from "the land that is not very far off;" and when they again communed together with their Lord, he bent so low to hear them, that it seemed to us who knelt by almost the mount of transfiguration. All the next day, as he lay on his lounge, he lived over that hour. Some one remarked that the bishop knew what topic would be acceptable to him. He answered, with a humorous face, "Why, if Bishop Foss had spent the hour in my room last night in rehearsing his European plans, I should have thought him insane." On Tuesday afternoon the kind bishop came again, with Mrs. Foss, and again the theme was "Jesus and the resurrection;" and when he finally commended his dying friend to God, to "our Elder Brother, *his* Brother, *my* Brother," there came a sense of security and blissful rest that never left him afterward.

The next day, — the day preceding the "day of prayer for colleges," — he asked if I should think him wild if he should say he was wondering if he could not be carried to the college chapel to-morrow, so he might talk, "just for a few minutes," in the prayer-meeting. He said, "I do so long to talk to the students once more! I want to try to impress them with the importance of the Christian life. I want them to see as I see it from my present stand-point. It is strange to me that so much of my work has been done from a sense of duty. Oh, if I could work now, I should work from a real, warm love for the Master and his cause. It seems to me I could convince everybody of the reality and blessedness of the Christian faith." When convinced he could not go, he wondered if he could meet the students in the parlors at home. For a few hours he indulged the pleasant thought; then he said, "I am afraid I could not endure it. My emotion would overcome me, and my strength would fail. No, I can only speak to one and another separately, as they call to see me." Nothing gave him more pleasure than the occasional visits from his former pupils.

On Thursday, the 28th, he spent much time in prayer for the blessing of God upon the day, and watched eagerly for some one to tell him how the meetings at college were resulting.

In the afternoon Dr. Hunt, who had preached in college chapel in the morning, called. His words of greeting were, "I wanted to come and congratulate you upon being so near the heavenly home." It was a welcome keynote. Mr. Harrington readily took it up, and for a half-hour he exulted in a conversation that led him almost out of sight of bodily ills; and the prayer that followed, to "our Father, our Saviour, our Comforter," brought answer of abiding joy.

The following night was one of great suffering, but, in the midst of one of the severest paroxysms of coughing, I noticed a particularly bright expression flit over his face. It seemed like a light reflected on him. I said at once, "Calvin, what is it?"—"I'll tell you as soon as I can," said he, smiling; and, when he was able to talk, he said, "My hard coughing made me know I could not stand such racking much longer, and the thought came to me, 'Soon people will be saying, "He is dead."' I thought how, in my old home, the word would go from one to another, 'Calvin Harrington is dead.' Then the thought came, 'But *I* shall be saying, *No, not dead; I am alive forevermore.*'" Then he dwelt most exultantly upon the "bliss of immortality," "life eternal." He said, "I fully *believe* that I shall *live forever;*" and he praised God for the glorious hope.

Another night, between fearful spasms of coughing, he said, "I have been thinking what a glorious offset this doctrine of the resurrection is, to the difficulty we have of comprehending God. I have been troubled, for a day or two, with the thought of the *eternity* of God. How can we conceive of a Being without beginning, without end, without cause? We cannot take it in, and I have been struggling against the doubts it suggests. But just now the *resurrection* of *Jesus* came to me, and that matches it."

CHAPTER XIV.

HEMORRHAGE. — PRAYER. — DAILY ROUTINE. — LETTERS. — HYMNS. — CALLS. — APPROACH OF DEATH. — DIRECTIONS. — MESSAGES. — LAST PRAYER-MEETING. — LAST SLEEP. — "INTO THOSE MANSIONS." — KINDNESS OF FRIENDS. — MEMORIAL OF FACULTY.

DURING the night of Saturday, Jan. 30, he had his first hemorrhage. It was slight in the beginning, but increased rapidly, and was apparently the breaking-up of a deep-seated pulmonary ulcer. This drew heavily on his little remaining strength, so we all saw he was going down with increased rapidity. For two or three days he conversed but little. On Sunday he said, " I will not try to talk any until Mr. —— comes [a student who had promised to call on that afternoon], so I may save all my strength for a little time with him. I want, if possible, to induce him to become an out-spoken Christian."

From the night of Aug. 10, 1852, it had been our invariable custom to unite our evening prayers at the bedside. Monday evening, Feb. 1, lying in his bed, paler and weaker than ever before, he prayed with unusual fervor, and for so many objects, — the Church he loved, the especial state of it here, the missionary of the cross, the preachers of God's word everywhere, the college, the professors, the students, Bishop Foss and family upon the deep, Dr. Hunt, and several others who had especially asked his prayers, his own kindred, — all were remembered with such an earnestness of desire, as if he had just then an especial audience with the Deity, and hastened to put in all his pleas, with the certain knowledge that they would be regarded. Then, oh, how tenderly! he prayed for me and "the dear ones at Wilbraham."

I said, when he ceased, "O Calvin, what can I do when I can no longer have your prayers?" Heb. i. 14 coming to mind just at the moment, I quoted it. "*Yes, yes,*" said he, "you have that text, and you have this, 'Thy Maker is thy husband;' and this, 'Let thy widows trust in me;' and oh, so many more precious promises! We don't know whether I am to go soon, but I think my failing strength these last few days squints that way. I wish I could sing!" and, with great effort, he sang the lines, —

"We shall see him as he is
By and by, when he comes;
We shall see him as he is,
When he comes."

It was his last song before Jesus came to lead him into that great company who sing around the throne.

The next day he wished to be brought down-stairs, saying, "I don't like to give up entirely until I am compelled to do so." He lay on the lounge in the parlor, and looked again on all the familiar home scenes. With help, he walked once more to the dining-room, and ate his last dinner at the family table. But the day was a very weary one, and the next morning he said calmly, he thought "he would not try to leave his room any more."

Most of the remaining time was spent in bed. Towards evening each day, he was helped to an easy-chair, where he sat about two hours, resting, eating his supper, and attending family prayers. For a week he prayed each time himself; the effort becoming too great for him, he called the last week on other members of the family. During the first of these two weeks, he saw very little company, but tried to rest, and conscientiously used every means for health, as if he knew it might be available. After his morning toilet, his breakfast, and an hour's rest, he listened daily to his own selections from the Bible, and his favorite hymns. Then he conversed a while on what had been read, and often his thoughts seemed to reach out into the unseen, and he would lie apparently rapt in a delightful communion with the Comforter. After this he invariably called for the reading of the daily paper, and listened with interest to all the secular news, commenting upon it with the same interest as if he were in active life. Then followed a time of quiet, a sort of half-dozing, for some time before dinner. One day at this hour I thought him asleep, and was very quiet, so as not to disturb his rest. At last he opened his eyes full of humor, and said, "You need not go tipping around any longer; I have not been asleep." I said, "What have you been doing?"—"Get your tablet, and I'll tell you," said he. When I was ready, he dictated four stanzas of a little poem, the first five of which he had written in a similar way a week before. When I expressed approval, and said, "I'll send it to the paper," he replied, "If you do, I'll whip you; I only made it to keep myself busy, and it is not worth printing at all. Now, remember, don't let any of these things that I have written in my weak condition ever see the light. If you are foolish enough to enjoy them, you can have them."

He received many letters from friends, which were sources of great comfort. He had frequently been called upon to sing some selection at funeral services. This he esteemed a sacred privilege. One morning he received a letter from a neighbor, in which, after referring to two such occasions, the writer said, "The hymns you sang in the Spirit never left me. God was calling after me, one of his children, but out in the world, — through you. I cannot remember any thing for a number of years that took hold of my soul like those hymns. I desire to say some word from God that will comfort or help you, as, in times past, you were used in helping me. You are near the entrance of that new life. Christ says, 'Whosoever believeth in me shall never die.' Hear Rev. i. 5, 6; 2 Pet. i. 16, 17, 18; 1 Pet. iv. 12, 13; 1 Pet. i. 1–4; Rom. viii. 37, 38, 39; John xiv. 26, 27." As these passages were read, Mr. Harrington said, "It seems to me, brother N—— must have been inspired to quote these special passages for me in just this order, they give me such new light and strength."

The next day a letter came from one of the patients of the insane-hospital, saying, "Your voice I have heard with delight preaching the blessed gospel of God's dear Son." This filled his heart with grateful joy, for though he had taken his turn with clergymen of the city in supplying the pulpit of the hospital very willingly, as a reasonable duty, yet he often feared that those to whom the preaching was especially directed were too much diseased to derive any real good. He rejoiced that God had allowed him to cheer at least one of those afflicted ones. There were other letters, for which, more than all, he thanked God with great joy. These were from former students of the university, one of whom he had often mourned over, and prayed for with great longing, but with disappointed hope. The assurance that his words, though apparently unheeded, had not been in vain, gave him great comfort.

On Thursday, the 11th, he lay very quiet for some time, when I asked for his thoughts. "I was thinking," said he, "of three hymns. Of that one by Ganse, — the 283d of the Hymnal, — especially of the last stanza: —

> 'Tell me much of cleansing blood;
> Show me sin, but sin forgiven;
> Step by step where Christ has trod,
> Help me home to heaven.'

"Then the 220th, by Charles Wesley: —

> 'O Love Divine, what hast thou done?
> The incarnate God hath died for me!
> The Father's co-eternal Son
> Bore all my sins upon the tree!
> The Son of God for me hath died.
> My Lord, my Love, is crucified!'

"I have been trying," said he, "to find one on the other side to match these, — a response of the human to the divine love. The only one I can think of, as coming anywhere near what I want, is this of Watts's, the 211th: —

> 'Were the whole realm of nature mine,
> That were a present far too small;
> Love so amazing, so divine,
> Demands my soul, my life, my all.'"

A Christian friend called to inquire for him. When told she was down-stairs, he said, "Give sister W—— my love; and tell her it is all bright here now, and when we get *over there* it will be brighter."

He suffered every day more from difficulty of breathing and from extreme restlessness. On Friday Professor Van Vleck came in, and was, as always, most welcome. Mr. Harrington was greatly cheered by the faithfulness of his colleagues, and sometimes wondered that his long sickness did not exhaust their sympathy. He told Professor Van Vleck of his intense unrest. Then he added cheerfully, "But though the exterior is so restless, the interior is very restful. Professor, it is *all* rest *within*." A little later Professor Rice came and talked with him a while. Soon Mr. Harrington said, "Professor, I should like to hear you pray once more. I may have several opportunities, we can't tell, but I should like to hear you now." And most comforting were the words of praise and supplication offered to God. As Professor Rice rose, he said, "Before you go, tell me about those Seney bonds. A paragraph in the paper to-day looked as though they had appreciated again." And the confirmation of this good news for the college was just as pleasing as if he had been, as of old, identified with all the work of the university. The full conviction that he was near the end of earthly life detracted nothing from his appreciation of the importance of it. Life was to him the workshop where the great Master-Builder had placed his workmen, and there was nothing of the work given them to do that was not worth earnest and careful attention until they were called away to other service.

All these nights he alternated between severe fits of

coughing, and moments of broken, heavy, tiresome sleeping. He talked almost constantly in his sleep, often fancying himself away on a journey, and piteously begging to go home. Once he called out so joyfully, "After all, here we are home in the midst of friends. Praise the Lord!" Waking or sleeping, he repeated passage after passage of Scripture, and many a favorite hymn, and often prayed with great earnestness. His last audible prayer in his sleep was on the night of Feb. 13, and was very distinct and coherent, ending formally with, "And now forgive us all our sins, and accept all our thanksgivings, for Jesus Christ's sake. Amen." The previous day, — Saturday, — after listening to a chapter from the Gospel of John, he said, "Now read me one of brother N——'s quotations, — the one from Peter." I began the one in 2d Peter. "No, no, not that, — the long one in the first chapter of 1st Peter. Read sixteen verses." As I read, he responded frequently with praises; and when I ended, he said, "How full that is of strong doctrines!" calling my attention to the fact that in those few verses the doctrines of the atonement, the resurrection, salvation, and eternal life in Jesus Christ, and his second advent, were all set forth.

Karl came at noon, and much of the afternoon was spent in company with him. On Sunday morning he enjoyed listening to the sound of the organ in the room below, as Karl played at family prayers; and said, when he went to him afterward, "Though I could not distinguish the words, I could easily follow the music, and knew they were, 'Abide with me.'"

That day he repeated with emphasis the last two lines of Philip Doddridge's hymn: —

"And crowned with victory, at his feet
I'll lay my trophies down."

My sister, sitting by, said, "Lay your burdens down?"

"No, no; not *burdens*, but *trophies*," he replied. A little after, he said, "I am resting on a firm foundation. There is nothing in all this world so solid, so immovable, so satisfactory, as the faith of our Lord Jesus Christ. Why, I *know* I am safe in him. The Word of God says, 'Him that cometh unto me, I will in no wise cast out.' I have fulfilled the conditions, — I have come to him, and he keeps his word. The everlasting arms are under me. If there is a God, he is a God of truth. His word cannot fail. And that there is a God *I know*.

"I have not the least fear or dread of death. Death is only the step over from this life into the life eternal.

"I used to think the things about me, that I could see and hear and feel by physical sense, were the real, tangible things; but now I see spiritual things are the only real ones."

When evening came we thought him unable to sit up; but he pleaded, "I shall sleep better if I am in my chair for a while; after a rest the night will be less tedious."

He had not led in family devotions for some days; but after taking his supper, he said, "Now, Karl, if you will read a very short Psalm, I will try to pray." Karl read the 121st, then his father prayed. Oh, how he prayed! It was evidently a great effort for his lungs, but his voice was almost unnaturally loud as he for the last time performed the priest's office at his own family altar. Such I know he felt to be the case, as one by one he committed us all to God, and consecrated himself, his family, all our interests for time and eternity, to the great Father of us all. We felt we were laid on the altar, and for Jesus' sake God accepted the offering.

The prayer ended, he was helped to bed; and then he said, "Now, let me rest while you and Karl eat supper; then I want to talk a little."

He was waiting for us, when in a few minutes we returned, and sat close by his bedside.

He began in trembling tones, and went back over his own life, tracing the wonderful leading hand of God in it all. He spoke of his early doubts in reference to a call to the ministry, — the question that so long troubled him, whether he ought to be in the active pastorate instead of a professor's chair. He expressed his final settled conviction, that for him the latter position was one in which there was even a greater opportunity for Christian influence and labor than anywhere else. He spoke of his great satisfaction that he had lived to see his son established in this calling, and should leave him knowing he was where he had great opportunity to work for Christ. That, he said, was the work of life. He was ambitious that his boy should be fully equipped for his earthly work. He wished him to use every facility to make and keep himself thoroughly qualified for all the demands of this growing age, and to use all his energy to make himself successful in his department of teaching. "But remember always," said he, " that there is a still higher goal to aim at, a far more important work to be accomplished. And wherever you are, let the spiritual welfare of those about you lie deepest in your heart."

He spoke of his hopes for Karl's domestic happiness, and his pleasure that the chosen one was a child of God, and worker for Jesus. He said, "I should have been very glad to live until your wedding-day," but with a smile added, "When it comes, Karl, I think I shall know about it. I *think* I shall be *there*."

He dwelt then much on his own strong confidence in God and in the Christian religion. He said, "I would be a Christian, if it were only for the joy it gives in this life;" and talked much of his great delight in the presence of the Comforter now.

He said then, "I am perfectly at rest in reference to my future. I know I am safe in Christ. We don't know what the future joys will be, but I think 'I shall be satisfied when I awake with his likeness.'"

He rejoiced greatly that we all rested on the same rock; that he could leave his dear ones, knowing that the same God who had so wonderfully led him all his life, and blessed him fully, now it was closing, was the God in whom they trusted. He said, "In him you are safe. He will lead you, and I can leave you in his hands with perfect confidence that at all times 'the Lord will provide.'"

After talking more minutely on family matters, he said, "Well, I can't talk any longer; and it is just as well, for I believe I have said all I want to." He bade us good-night, and tried to rest. For an hour or two he slept somewhat quietly; then his breathing became more difficult, the coughing more constant, and suffering more evident. The last part of the night, his feet became cold. He said, "Don't try to warm them, they do not feel cold to me." He knew evidently that it was the chill that could never be removed. When morning came, he said, "Karl must go to his work this morning. He is needed at Wilbraham; and though I love to have him here, I ought not to keep him from his duties, as there is nothing he can do to relieve me."

So their last kisses were exchanged, and good-bys said, while the death-angel waited.

Then he went through his usual morning programme, not omitting the listening to the daily paper. About eleven he sank rapidly, and for a few moments was unable to speak, and we thought we had listened to his last words. But restoratives were administered, and he came back to us. His physicians, who were out of town at that hour, returned about two in the afternoon. A glance told them the truth, and with few words they left the room.

As I went back to Mr. Harrington, after a few moments' conversation with them, he asked, "What did they tell you?" I said, "Do you remember saying to me a few days ago, that you would like to go home then, if it were God's will?" — "Yes." — "And do you feel just so still? Do you want to go to-day?" — "If I could live a year longer to preach and sing and pray, and *work for souls*, I would love to live. But I had to give that up some time ago; and since I can only live to suffer, and cause suffering and care for others, I would rather go. Yes, I would like to go to-day." I told him his physicians thought he could live but a few hours longer. He closed his eyes, and for some moments was evidently prayerfully taking in the momentous fact. Then he whispered, "*Praise the Lord!*"

Soon he said, "You have been writing some letters to-day. Will you read me a sample?" I read one. It was only a word to prepare his near relatives for the severe blow that must soon follow. "That is right," said he, and added, "You will have to send telegrams to-morrow. You had better prepare a list of names now, lest you may not be so well able to think of all later, and may neglect somebody." I told him I had already made a partial list. "Read me that," said he. I did so, and he added several names that he wished to have remembered. Then he spoke of other arrangements that should be made, quite as calmly as he would have spoken if the journey he was about to take were to London, instead of the heavenly city.

My sister, who had been with us for two months, lightening all our burdens, came into the room; and he called, "Minerva, the doctors say I am going soon. I want to say a few things to you that I shall not be able to say by and by. Give my love to all the kith and kin, and tell them I would be glad to answer all their letters separately, but they will get no more letters from me through the United States mail; but — 'Are they not all ministering spirits?'" Then he added, "You must hurry your letter, so to have it go out in the next mail."

Said he, "I did mean to write to G—— myself, but I wish you would write for me. You know what I want to tell him. Tell him all about what a comfort this blessed religion is to me, and ask him to come to Jesus for the comfort he needs so much."

Of a friend whom he highly esteemed, and for whom he had often prayed, he said, "I want him to be a believer in Jesus. What a power he would be for Christ! I want you to carry him this message from me. Carry it either by word of mouth or by letter, as you choose. Tell him *this from me :* 'Come to Jesus in his own way; come humbly, and consecrate the rest of your life and service to him, and let us enjoy the heavenly mansions together.'"

He heard familiar voices down-stairs. Said he, "The neighbors are coming in to inquire for me. Give them this message from me. Always say that I send Christian love to my neighbors, with a hope that we may be very close together in the heavenly world." Just at night his friend Professor Prentice came into his room. He had been expecting him, and looked up so glad, saying, "I want you to pray again with me." I said, "Wait a little. I want him to do something else before he prays." Mr. Harrington looked reprovingly, but I persisted: "You have taken no nourishment since one o'clock; and I think, after a glass of milk, you would enjoy the prayer better." — "I cannot; I cannot raise my head." — "But," I said, "I think Professor can lift you up." — "He couldn't do it," said he. "Why," said the kind friend, "I could do any thing for you, Professor;" and, lifting him in his arms, he held him firmly while he drank his last earthly food. Then they talked of the "home over there," and the dear ones awaiting; and their prayers of faith once more went up together to the God they trusted. Their love had been cemented in sorrow, and death only fastened it more firmly.

This was the beginning of Mr. Harrington's last prayer-meeting; for soon Professor Van Benschoten followed, and tenderly committed the suffering one to the arms of the loving Jesus.

His pastor, Rev. W. V. Kelly, whose welcome visits had been very frequent during all his sickness, came in a little later, and once more prayed the Father for divine aid for his waiting servant. Words of comfort followed; and, as he was about to leave, Mr. Harrington said, "Tell me once more about the new church. I did hope I might live to see it completed, but I shall have to give that up." He had watched its progress daily, through the reports of friends, since the first brick was laid; and he did not forget it even when stepping upon the portal of the "house not built with hands."

Though consciously so near death, he lost no interest in the things about him, and even retained his old fondness for humor. Early in the night, when we tried to give him a swallow of water, he said, "Now, let me tell you just how I can take it. Put it away down by the side of the bed, so, as my head lies off, I can just touch my lips to the surface." And with a merry glance at a dear nephew sitting by, he said, "I guess Bing. has drank water out of a brook before now. He knows how we do it."

Between the hours of eleven and one, he suffered greatly. His position was continually changed, but he could find rest nowhere. His breathing grew more and more difficult, until I knew he feared, as I did, terrible agony at the last. He commenced a remark implying dread, but instantly checked it, and with earnestness repeated, " The Lord is my light and my salvation : whom shall I fear? The Lord is the strength of my life: of whom shall I be afraid?" He closed his eyes, evidently in prayer; and all my soul cried with him unto the Lord, " Take him not away in extreme suffering. I will hold him back no longer. Take him when thou wilt, only grant us this, that he may go peacefully." His restlessness ceased. Pressing my hand with all the energy of the death-grasp, he said, " Glory be to the Father, and to the Son, and to the Holy Ghost;" and our voices united for the last time in the words, "As it was in the beginning, is now, and ever shall be, world without end. Amen."

Then he fell into a quiet sleep. There was no more restlessness, no more expression or indication of suffering, no incoherent words; but as a little child sleeps in health, so he seemed to rest from the hour of two in the morning until six. Then he suddenly turned his head to one side, a few times gasped very lightly, and we saw that "he was not, for God had taken him." His eyes were closed as they had been during that last quiet sleep, and his own smile was on his lips.

Our prayers had been answered, and in gratitude my heart whispered, "The Lord gave, and the Lord hath taken away: blessed be the name of the Lord."

As I think of the last weeks of his suffering and weariness, exchanged for rest and triumph, these stanzas of one of his own hymns come to replace selfish longings by thanksgiving to our Father, who has given his beloved sleep : —

> Into those mansions pure and holy,
>   Cometh tears nor pain;
> Followers of the meek and lowly
>   Meet their Lord again.
> Singing are the angels, singing, singing,
>   In that sinless land;
> Ringing are the voices, ringing, ringing,
>   Voices of a sainted band.
>
> Sorrow and sighing from the immortal
>   Evermore are fled;
> Joyfully at the heavenly portal,
>   Shout the risen dead.

>Everlasting joy, all glorious, glorious,
>   On their heads shall be,
>Everlasting life, o'er death victorious,
>   Through a long eternity.

It would be a relief to my own heart if I could express at all adequately my gratitude to those who, in so many ways, blessed us during the days of my husband's sickness. The members of the university and their families, our pastor, and the members of our own church, neighbors and friends of every name, — these were not all. But many on whom we had not even the claim of acquaintance came to show their sympathy. Aged and infirm ones toiled feebly to our door to exchange words of Christian greeting, and little children brought their sweet smiles of cheer. The various tokens of kind remembrance caused the patient sufferer repeatedly to say, "It almost pays to be sick, so to learn the wealth of human sympathy."

His room was almost literally a flower-garden. He never failed to ask for the donor's name, and often feared his pleasure in the gifts would not be known. Once, when luscious fruits, tastefully arranged with flowers, were presented him, he exclaimed, with moistened eyes, "What shall I render unto the Lord for all his benefits? For surely, though the messengers who bring all these gifts are human, the real giver is Divine."

One morning in August, after looking about with pleasure on the profusion of fragrant flowers that brightened his room, a cloud came over his face, and he said, "Do you know what I dread? It is the time when these gifts will cease. These dear friends think that I am soon to leave them, and their kind sympathy is expressed in this abundance of flowers. But I dread the time when I shall have lived on and on, until they have become weary waiting, — for they *must* be absorbed in their own duties, — and I shall miss them." I suggested that this was the season of flowers, and the abundance now caused his friends comparatively little sacrifice, and doubtless gave them pleasure; but by and by, when the cold came, and the flowers withered, we would not expect them, and would know that the lack was not a change in our friends, whose sympathy surely was not limited by the flower-season. "I guess that is the right way to look at it," said he; "and so we will enjoy them while we can."

But the flowers never failed to come. The frosts came. Winter came with its cold and wind and snow. But flowers came too; and as the days grew colder, their presence was sweeter. Only a few days before he went away, a dear neighbor brought a lily in bud, whose development he watched with much interest, directing its position to favor the sun's rays and his own view; and when he closed his eyes to earth's beauties, the pure white lily was beside him.

After his spirit fled to the land of perennial flowers, these unfailing friends came to place the bright, sweet things he loved upon his bier, and to strew them on his grave. God bless them, and lead them up where he can tell them better how precious were their ministrations!

Among such kind memorials as those of the Prohibition Society of Middletown, the Xi Chapter of the Psi Upsilon Fraternity, and the Alumni of Wesleyan University, it seems peculiarly appropriate for that of the Faculty, in which he had been a brother for nearly a quarter of a century, to be inserted here : —

WESLEYAN UNIVERSITY, March 16, 1886.

"We desire to place upon the records of the Faculty an expression of our sense of the loss we have sustained as a Faculty, and of the yet deeper sense of loss we feel as individuals, in the death of our colleague and friend, Professor Calvin Sears Harrington. For nearly twenty-five years, Professor Harrington had been a member of this Faculty. He had proved himself an accurate and elegant scholar, a careful and successful teacher. In the punctual discharge of all his professorial duties, in his constant concern for all the interests of the college, and his unselfish devotion to its welfare, he was a model or us all.

"But it is as the friend and the Christian, that Professor Harrington will always be thought of first, and remembered longest. The moral and religious tone of the college community was to him a matter of constant solicitude. It is probable that he was not absent from his Thursday-evening religious class-meeting more than half a dozen times in twenty years (except when he was out of town) ; and it was very seldom indeed that he failed to be present at the students' prayer-meeting on sabbath mornings ; while his own daily religious life was a guide and inspiration to all who knew him. His character was so sincere, and his disposition so kindly, that it is doubtful whether he ever gave offence to a pupil in his life ; and it seems certain that no student could pass under the influence of his presence for four years without being deeply impressed by the gracious charm of his character.

"To a degree very rare he united positiveness of conviction with gentleness of manner, strictness of moral principle with kindness for the individual. In the counsels of the Faculty it used to be frequently noticed, when matters of discipline were under discussion, that no one would insist on so high and strict a rule of conduct for the student, but that no one was so forbearing and hopeful in his dealing with the individual offender.

"Only those who had the privilege of knowing Professor Harrington intimately, as most of us had, can understand the rare social charm of his character. A native courtesy and gentleness, a winning unselfishness and kindness of disposition, an active intelligence, and a cultivated taste, a peculiar, ever-present humor, made all the more irresistible by a certain demureness of manner, — all these qualities combined to make Professor Harrington one of the most congenial of companions, as well as one of the truest of friends.

"All the traits of mind and heart that won our admiration and love during the years of his active association with us, were only heightened and intensified during the months of weakness and weariness that preceded his death. And, now that he is gone, we find the memory of him a constant inspiration; and as we think of him we say, — higher praise no man can give, — 'He was a Christian gentleman.'"

www.ingramcontent.com/pod-product-compliance
Lightning Source LLC
Chambersburg PA
CBHW032157160426
43197CB00008B/950